INVERCLYDE

FEEPAME

REFRAME

HOW TO SOLVE THE WORLD'S TRICKIEST PROBLEMS

Eric Knight

\B b\

Biteback Publishing

First published in Australia in 2012 by Black Inc.,
an imprint of Schwartz Media Pty Ltd.

This edition published in Great Britain in 2012 by
Biteback Publishing Ltd
Westminster Tower
3 Albert Embankment
London
SE1 7SP
Copyright © Eric Knight 2012

ISBN 978-1-84954-332-3

10 9 8 7 6 5 4 3 2 1

A CIP catalogue record for this book is available from the British Library.

Set in Fleischmann by Peter Long

Printed and bound in Great Britain by
CPI Group (UK) Ltd, Croydon CR0 4YY

For my mother and father,
with love and gratitude

WHY PEOPLE ARE SMART

but act so dumb

I first realised I was missing a part of the world during the summer I spent in the jungles of Costa Rica. Hidden beneath the giant arms of the ceiba tree, I felt at peace. Costa Rica offered my twenty-year-old self a refuge from the pace of the modern world. There was a thrill that came with anonymity. I had spent my first two years of university learning Spanish and, with a carefully cultivated tan, I now delighted in being mistaken as *tico*. I loved bartering with locals at the market for fruit and vegetables. I savoured the simple taste of *gallo pinto*, rice with beans. Whenever I could, I would carry a day's supplies in a small string bag. The idea that I might get lost and be able to survive on the bare necessities was my ultimate escapist dream.

In Costa Rica I was posted to a little village called Grano de Oro as a volunteer aid worker with a group of eleven other Australians and Canadians. Grano de Oro, we were told, needed a community hall. The Cabécars, the local indigenous people, would rest there after days of journeying through dense jungle before making their way to the regional markets in Turrialba. The hall would offer shelter and a chance to mingle. Every few months the US government organised a helicopter drop of food, toys, clothes and other supplies at a spot nearby. The hall would also make it easier to distribute these things up into the mountains.

Our modest mission that summer never happened. The building materials for the hall never arrived. Warm tropical rain set in and the road into the mountains became impossibly treacherous. Bored and restless to change the world, I began spending more time at the *pulpería*, the corner shop where people from the village and the mountains hung out and played pool. As my Spanish improved and the people at the *pulpería* went from being strangers to friends, I learnt something that profoundly changed the way I saw the world.

The thing was, no one in Grano de Oro wanted this community hall. They wouldn't say no if you offered it to them for free, but they already had one which more than did the job. The reason they had signed the government papers and what they really wanted was people to help mentor the kids in their community – the ones my age. The world was changing and these kids were missing out on the benefits of economic progress. Solving the economic challenges facing Grano de Oro was more complicated than building a new community hall. But seeing this required more patience and a different approach than first met the eye.

As I went to the *pulpería* day after day, playing more pool than I liked and speaking more Spanish than I knew how, I began to realise that my Costa Rican friends didn't want the life I had imagined for them. It did them no favours to put up a few planks or clean up their gardens so they could grow vegetables and settle into life in the jungle.

When I asked them what they wanted to do with their lives, their answers shocked me. Alejandro wanted to become an accountant. Henry wanted to be a banker or a businessman. Nazareth wanted to study international relations, and the rest wanted to be lawyers.

"Why on earth would you want to do that?" I asked them indignantly. "I've tried it, and believe me, what you've got is much better." It was only later that I realised the mistake I was making. In projecting my own dreams for them, I was robbing them of the freedom to have their own.

Solving the economic challenges of Grano de Oro was about education and mentoring, not about building something you could bounce a ball against or take a photo of. The building was an obvious answer to Grano's problems, but it wasn't the best one. My friends eventually went to university in San Jose, but I was the one who learnt the lesson that summer. By seeing the problem from one angle, I had missed the answers lying just out of view.

1.

This is a book about our trickiest problems, how they have answers, and why we miss them. I'm interested in political and economic problems, mainly. In the chapters ahead we will travel through history: from the spectacular financial bubbles which plagued Dutch finance in the seventeenth century to Lawrence of Arabia's great campaigns in the Middle East, from the fears of ecological catastrophe in eighteenth-century England to the flow of Mexican migrants crossing the US border every day. Each of these problems is very different, but I want to persuade you that we make the same mistake in each case. We focus on what's immediately apparent and we miss the bigger picture.

To see what I mean, take a look at the drawing below. It is a picture of a table resting against a wall, with several objects sitting on it: a box of pins, a candle and some matches. How would you light the candle and attach it to the wall so that no wax drips onto the table?

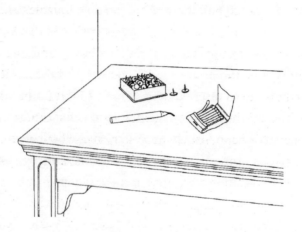

Don't worry if you find this tricky. The experiment was invented more than half a century ago by Karl Duncker, a German psychologist, to examine the way we think through puzzles. The most common answer is to pin the candle to the wall at an angle so that the wax runs down the wall. The correct answer is to empty the box of pins and use it as a candleholder. When you pin the box to the wall and place the candle inside, there is no risk of wax splashing on the table.

The Duncker candle problem isn't an intelligence test. It

doesn't reflect how well educated you are or how big your brain is. Young children are among the best at getting the right answer. The reason we struggle with it is that we are so used to seeing the box in terms of one purpose – as a container for pins – that we miss the other way of using it. Once the solution is revealed to us, we get it. No one makes the same mistake twice with the Duncker candle problem. You will now never forget to see a box of pins as a potential candleholder.

The Duncker problem is a neat party trick. But in this book I want to pull it out of the realm of puzzles and apply it to the world of politics. My contention is that we often struggle with our trickiest political problems because of how we see them. We tend to view the world in set ways. We become so intent on analysing a problem one way that we lose all the subtlety needed to get to the best answer. When this happens, we need to readjust how we interpret the world around us. We can solve seemingly insoluble problems by changing the way we think about them.

I am aware this is an optimistic – some would even say simplistic – view of the world. I'll justify it as the book goes on. But to fully appreciate why we miss the answers latent in the world around us, we need to go one step beyond the Duncker experiment. It's not just that we fixate on one thing and not others. It's that we fixate on *certain kinds* of things. Let me show you what I mean.

Suppose for a moment that you are a randomly selected person living in the United States in 2006. Think about what you know of the place and ask yourself the following question: which of the following is most likely to kill you next year? Take a close look at each line and select which cause of death, in column "A" or "B", is more likely in each case.

CAUSES OF DEATH	
A	**B**
All accidents (unintentional injuries)	Stroke
Suicide	Diabetes
High blood pressure	Influenza and pneumonia
Homicide	Alzheimer's disease
War	Syphilis

If you answered "A" to any of the options above, you have illustrated the point I am about to make. These causes of death are taken from the records of the US National Center for Health Statistics for 2007. In each case, the likelihood of being killed by "B" is higher than for "A". In fact, in almost every case the likelihood of "B" outnumbers "A" by a factor of at least two to one.

The reason why many of us were drawn to column "A" is because it contains all the causes of death we are most likely to see and hear about. We have all read stories of people who committed suicide, but deaths by diabetes rarely make the papers. Some of our relatives probably suffer from high blood pressure, and it seems a whole lot worse than when they last had the flu. As for murder and war, they are the stuff of the nightly news.

Two cognitive psychologists working in the 1970s, Amos Tversky and Daniel Kahneman, conducted an experiment much like the one above. They went through a list of causes of death with interview subjects and recorded their reactions. We will learn more about Tversky and Kahneman's work in Chapter 1, but their conclusions were basically this: people overestimated the likelihood of certain causes of death – murder, suicide, fatal accidents – because these were the most dramatic and easy to see. What they underestimated were the silent killers – asthma, stroke and so on.

In the chapters ahead, I call this impulse the *magnifying glass trap*. Most people think of a magnifying glass as a visual aid, but I think of it in the opposite way. The magnifying glass trap is the tendency to zoom in and fix on one corner of the universe and miss those elements of a solution lying just outside the lens. Sometimes we are lured into the trap by shiny objects: those parts of a problem which are visually compelling and graphic. At other times we are lured by intellectual trinkets and shiny ideas. Both can distract us on our mission to solve complex problems. It's only when we cast them aside that we have a chance of making progress.

2.

I've presented two ideas so far. One: we tend to view the world through a magnifying glass. Two: we tend to point the magnifying glass in the direction of shiny objects. These ideas should prompt you to ask a very good question. If we look for the answers in the wrong places, what should we do about it?

I will suggest in this book that we should "reframe" the problem. It is important to be clear what I mean by this. Reframing is not a linguistic tool, a trick to disguise or evade difficult problems. Rather, it is an intellectual choice we must make. Seeing the answer to our problem requires us to have the right elements of the problem – the right system – in focus. Instead of a magnifying glass, think for a moment of the lens on a camera. When the aperture is set at one width, we see a flower. That's one system in focus. Widen the aperture and we see a meadow – that's another system in focus. Widen it further and we see the mountains – a third system. Having a particular system in focus alters our ability to see the answer. Focus on the flower, and the mountains are invisible. Reframe the problem – remove the magnifying glass – and we may arrive at the right answer.

In the chapters ahead I will reframe some of our most intractable political debates. I will be ambitious in choosing what we take on: the biggest political headaches of the last decade. We will begin by looking at the way a Wall Street banker did a deal in the late '90s. We will also examine how a US general fought a war in the Middle East. We will consider climate change, immigration and more. In each case, these debates have become stuck because someone has fallen into the magnifying glass trap.

Reframe is as much a book about human psychology as it is about politics. I'm less interested in telling you what to think and more interested in showing you an alternative way to approach sticky situations. In the end the story I will tell is an optimistic one of how we can make the world more peaceful and prosperous. We *can* resolve our trickiest problems. In some cases we already are solving them – we just don't see it. The most common mistake is to search for the answers in the wrong place without thinking to adjust our point of view. Sometimes this mistake is made by others. In this book I want us to ask a different question: when is the mistake our own?

CHAPTER 1

THE WALL STREET BANKER GENE
and why we all have it

When Robert Merton and Myron Scholes accepted the Nobel Prize for Economics in late 1997, they were already waist-deep in one of the most spectacular crashes of modern finance. The pair were awarded the prize for their work in financial mathematics. Their accomplishment? A tool to model complex financial products. Globalisation had opened up highways for money to flow across borders faster than ever before, but to all intents and purposes the money was invisible.

Merton and Scholes's models were installed in the engine room of Wall Street's most exclusive hedge fund, Long-Term Capital Management. By late 1998, the fund had collapsed. The real story of LTCM's demise was a surprising one. More important than the amount of money lost were the implications for financial modelling. Merton and Scholes had treated history as if it was a sequence of events to which savvy traders reacted, but it turned out that the world was more complicated than that. The problem was that the LTCM models were more like a magnifying glass than a mirror. They zoomed in on micro events on the trading floor, but they missed the powerful macroeconomic processes at play in the global economy.

Before going any further, it's worth noting what a big deal LTCM was. The fund was run by a high-finance dream team. John Meriwether, a legendary bond trader at Salomon Brothers in the 1980s, was its executive director. The team he put together was hand-picked from Salomon Brothers when it collapsed in the 1990s. The rest were ex-faculty members from Harvard Business School and MIT. Merton and Scholes sat on the board of directors. When the fund finally came together in 1994, it was oversubscribed to the tune of billions of dollars. America's richest people, associated through firms like Merrill Lynch and UBS, the investment banks, lined out the door for a chance to put their dollars to work in the fund. It didn't take long for LTCM to become one of the biggest private money-making machines in history.

The package LTCM offered its investors was known as fixed-income arbitrage. It was the ultimate investment opportunity: maximum return, minimum risk. It worked like this: computers were programmed to scan the markets for potentially attractive investments. If two assets were found which were virtually identical but traded at different prices in different parts of the world, the fund bought the cheaper asset and squeezed out a profit from the difference in market prices. The strategy worked because these discrepancies were hard to find and usually too small for ordinary investors to take advantage of. With its superior technology and number-crunching ability, LTCM backed itself to find the anomalies before anyone else and exploit them ruthlessly.

LTCM described itself as a market-neutral fund. In other words, it promised to make investors money no matter what the state of the market – up or down – or the performance of any particular asset class – stocks, bonds and so on. This feat was possible because instead of picking a particular asset (for example, sub-prime mortgages in the United States) and making money from its spectacular ascent, LTCM made money when the same asset was traded at different prices.

When the fall came, it was swift. On Friday 21 August 1998, LTCM lost $550 million in a single day. Over a four-month period that year, LTCM lost close to half its value, wiping out US$4.6 billion in investor capital. Reeling from the losses, John Meriwether wrote a letter to investors on 2 September asking for emergency capital to carry the fund through a difficult time. News of the letter swept Wall Street. The amount of money at stake was so large that when the New York Federal Reserve heard what was happening, it paid the fund a visit. On 20 September, Peter Fisher, the executive vice-president of the New York Federal Reserve, some of his colleagues from the US Federal Reserve and a string of bankers from Goldman Sachs and JP Morgan turned up at the fund's New Haven offices. They asked to inspect the books. What they discovered was extraordinary.

The model which LTCM had been peddling was known in the finance industry as "relative betting". The "relative" part referred to the fact that there were two almost identical assets. The "betting" was the assumption that the prices would eventually converge, ensuring a profit for the holder of the lower-priced asset. In theory, this would always happen over the long term, which in the world of finance meant roughly every seven years. Over the very long term, however, history showed that markets crashed on average once a decade. And when the crash came, it didn't matter what *relative* positions existed in the market. All assets in the market went down.

LTCM's troubles had started in May 1998, when the Asian financial crisis spurred a sell-off in American and European stock markets. By August the contagion had spread to bond markets after the Russian government, weakened by political unrest and flagging oil prices, defaulted on its debts. But instead of adjusting for these long-term trends, the brains behind LTCM bet on their ability to outfox the market. Instead of unwinding the fund's investment positions, they doubled up and leveraged to the hilt. It was the wrong move: by the time Fisher and his intervention team arrived in September 1998, LTCM was exposed to debt thirty times its capital base. It needed more than emergency capital. It needed a cash injection the size of the GDP of a small country.

The lesson of LTCM was that its bosses had the wrong system in focus. By reacting to recent events, they had ignored long-run processes. LTCM's managers had been so confident of their ability to beat history that they had not sufficiently stress-tested their financial tools. According to Niall Ferguson, the British economic historian, had they plugged as little as a decade's worth of data into their models before setting out, they would have realised the weak point in their strategy. They had failed to turn to history. "If I had lived through the Depression," Meriwether later said, "I would have been in a better position to understand events."

1.

What is the *precise* mistake the people at LTCM made? Ignorance about the future is an age-old problem, so they can hardly be blamed for that. Nor can you fault the conclusions they drew from the data flickering across their computer screens. Given what they knew about converging asset prices, it made sense to hold onto their investments.

The error in judgement happened at the very start of the investment process. It came from the data they chose to feed into the system and rely on when making their decisions. By taking a small strip of history and plugging it into their model, they were reacting to short-term anomalies and not long-term trends. Long-Term Capital Management's mistake was, ironically enough, to not think long-term enough.

There is nothing original about the punchline that someone on Wall Street was short-term in their thinking. But you'll be glad to know that that is not my punchline. What's more interesting, indeed truly remarkable, about the LTCM story is that *these* people should have fallen into the short-term trap. These were intelligent, well-educated, rational people who were specifically employed for their ability to avoid losses of just this kind. It would be easy to say that greed and a passion for making money got the better of them, but that is manifestly untrue.

Michael Lewis noted in a *New York Times* article in 1999 that the most conspicuous form of consumption among the "young professors" at LTCM was to reinvest their bonuses back into improving their model. Intellectual accuracy, in other words, was the ultimate prize. These were some of the most conservative economic thinkers and academics of their time. They had every incentive to make the right decisions. "When you asked them a simple question," Lewis wrote, "they thought about it for eight months before they answered, and then their answer was so complicated you wished you had never asked." To the extent that they were vulnerable to emotion and human error, their models were designed to detect and eliminate this. That they failed so spectacularly needs more than a little explaining. Let's go back in time, fifty years earlier, to try to solve this riddle.

In the 1950s, economists trying to understand how people made decisions about things as simple as buying food at the supermarket, or as complex as buying shares on the stock market, referred to something called the "pigeon puzzle". The pigeon puzzle was an experiment involving a pigeon and a series of incentives and punishments. When the pigeon did an approved task, it was rewarded with food. When it did a disapproved one, it received an electric shock. The conclusion of the pigeon puzzle was that pigeons tried to optimise outcomes, responding to the carrots and sticks. They tried to maximise their gains and minimise their losses. The pigeon was, in other words, a perfectly rational being.

As the Cold War engulfed the second half of the twentieth century, a key political debate was how best to organise human society. The question was a simple one. Were people like pigeons? Was it fair to assume that people were rational and able to allocate resources optimally in a market economy? Or was it safer to rely on a paternal government to organise how things were produced and distributed?

The answer? To a large extent people were rational. Unlikely as it might sound, a society governed by incentives and punishments resulted in a fairer allocation of resources than a socialist society ruled by benevolent dictate. Because people were rational, they were able to make choices in a marketplace which optimised their social outcomes, such as finding the right person to marry or buying fashionable clothes. The end result was that almost everyone was better off.

There was, however, a small catch. The assumption that people were pigeons could not account for the occasional, seemingly random moments of demonstrably bad human judgement. If people were so smart, why did they sometimes make decisions that were so dumb? If people always made the optimal choice, then why was the divorce rate so high? If we always chose in our best interest, why did some people have such demonstrably bad dress sense? The failure of LTCM was a case in point. It was in no one's interest to lose US$4.6 billion in four months, and yet history had a way of repeating when it came to such mistakes. Clearly, something was up.

The easy way of resolving the apparent contradiction was to argue that the starting assumption was wrong: people were in fact irrational. The better answer came from an economist at Carnegie Mellon University, Herb Simon. Simon spent his career unpicking the conundrum that people, though rational, sometimes made decisions which went against their best long-term interests. A contemporary of the legendary free-marketeers Milton Friedman and Gary Becker, Simon dedicated his Nobel Prize lecture in 1978 to outlining why their rational choice theory was not a complete explanation of reality. Like the pigeon puzzle, rational choice theory contended that people were perfectly capable of deciding what was in their own best interests without any assistance. The extension of this was that all people acting in their best interests benefited society as a whole. Simon's view was that the real world was a little more complicated.

In his opening remarks in Stockholm, Simon directed his audience to the words of the great nineteenth-century economist Alfred Marshall. Marshall had made the following observation: "Economics ... is on the one side a study of wealth; and on the other, and more important side, a part of the study of man." What was missing from Friedman and Becker's economics, Simon argued, was an appreciation of human psychology. Theirs was the story of *homo economicus*. It needed an extra chapter on *homo sapiens*.

The "sapiens", or thinking, part of Herb Simon's theory was important. Simon had not been awarded the Nobel

Prize for arguing that humankind was irrational. After all, neurologists and psychologists universally agreed that this was plainly wrong. The very fact that humankind had maintained itself for so many millennia was evidence that it was supremely rational. Self-preservation was a rational goal. Over the long run humans had done an exceptional job of securing and advancing their material self-interest. The problem, Simon argued, came down to how we reasoned our way through short-term events.

Simon's theory was called "bounded rationality". Its central claim was that although we were supremely rational, we tended to see the world through blinkers. Our ability to make decisions was "bounded" by various limits. There were limits on how much of the world we could see directly at any one time, the number of perspectives we could consider, our memory capacity, our level of expertise, and so on. These limits meant that we tended to solve complex problems by breaking them down and focusing on their most digestible parts. By using these intellectual shortcuts, people had a tendency to leave an awful lot of information out of the picture. Large tracts of the world remained outside the frame.

After inventing the notion of bounded rationality, Simon left it to others to add flesh through real-world experiments. Towards the end of his 1978 speech, Simon referred to two up-and-coming cognitive psychologists – Amos Tversky of Stanford University and Daniel Kahneman of Hebrew University, whom we met earlier – who had shown some promise in this regard. Tversky and Kahneman

19

used social experiments to drill down and examine the detail of Simon's theory.

In 2002, Kahneman was awarded a Nobel Prize for his contribution to a new field called behavioural economics. Through the 1980s and 1990s behavioural economists spent a lot of time examining the world of finance. Pointing out how the traders at LTCM fixated on small datasets to the exclusion of broader historical trends was the kind of research they did.

2.

The LTCM debacle showed that some well-paid Wall Street bankers viewed the world through a magnifying glass. Not too many surprises there. But the point behind the emerging academic discipline of behavioural economics was that it wasn't *just* Wall Street bankers who walked into the magnifying glass trap. We all did. Let me show you what I mean.

Linda is thirty-one years old, single, outspoken and very bright. She majored in philosophy at university. As a student, she was deeply concerned with issues of discrimination and social justice, and she also participated in anti-nuclear demonstrations. Which is more probable?

(1) Linda is a bank teller
(2) Linda is a bank teller and a committed feminist

Most of us answer (2), but it cannot possibly be more probable. Consider the mathematics of the question. The chance that Linda fulfils *both* conditions – that she is both a bank teller *and* a feminist – is always less than the chance that she fulfils just one condition – that she is a bank teller. But the question feeds our cognitive biases. We are inclined to fast answers based on what we have seen before. As soon as we see the words "social justice" and "feminist", we circle the second answer, forgetting to zoom out and consider the problem objectively. We leap to a conclusion, which can yield the wrong answer.

Let's try another one. Suppose I have just given you $1000 for participating in my experiment. Now I'm going to give you a choice. You can have either (a) a 50 per cent chance of winning another $1000 or (b) a guaranteed additional $500. Which would you prefer? Write the answer down.

Now clear your mind and answer a new question. Suppose you are on a quiz show and you have just won $2000. The host gives you an option in your final round. You can have either (c) a 50 per cent chance of losing $1000 or (d) a guaranteed loss of $500 and no more. Which option do you choose? Write down your second answer.

Tversky and Kahneman conducted an experiment similar to this in 1979 with two groups. One group answered the first question. Most people – 84 per cent – chose option (b), a guaranteed $500. The other group answered the second question and most people – 69 per cent – chose option (c), a 50–50 chance of losing $1000. The results are slightly distorted by asking you both questions in sequence, but the point should still be clear. The pay-off in both questions is identical, but our response to them is different. In both cases we have a 50 per cent probability of ending up with $2000 and a 100 per cent probability of ending up with $1500. But the majority of us react differently depending on whether the choice is presented as a win or as a loss. We are "risk-averse for positive prospects", but "risk-seeking for negative prospects".

Tversky and Kahneman ran many such experiments on well-educated people. What they discovered supported the view that we *all* view the world with certain built-in biases. They gave each of these biases a name. The Linda experiment showed the "conjunction fallacy", and the choice of different money options was called "prospect theory".

Then there was the "representativeness bias", the tendency to assume that the past predicted the future because recent events were fresh in our minds. At a roulette table, gamblers were likely to assume that red was more probable after a run of black. In fact, the probability of red or black each time was always 50–50. Our expectation was affected by what we had seen before. We assumed that the world had a way of balancing out the recent hot run of black, even though a new player to the table would never make this mistake.

In another case, people in one group gave a different estimate of the answer to the sum

$$8 \times 7 \times 6 \times 5 \times 4 \times 3 \times 2 \times 1 = ?$$

than did a second group when it was presented in a different way:

$$1 \times 2 \times 3 \times 4 \times 5 \times 6 \times 7 \times 8 = ?$$

The sums are, of course, identical, but to have "8" as your first impression yielded a larger estimate. The median estimate of the first group was 2250, whereas for the second group it was 512. The correct answer was 40,320.

In cases where individual choices made an enormous collective difference – such as in financial markets – Tversky and Kahneman's tools offered a new way of interpreting events. For four centuries merchants and speculators had ridden the waves of optimism and pessimism that gave rise to stock-market bubbles. Such bubbles had diverse causes and it was hard to explain them all by a single factor. You could see them as moments of mindless emotion: times when humans behaved with a herd instinct. Alternatively, as in the case of LTCM, they might be seen as mindful misjudgements.

If the first was true, then stock-market bubbles were unavoidable. But if the problem owed more to investors being drawn to the wrong elements of the problem – that is, placing the wrong system in focus – then the problem might be quelled over time, as investors learnt to readjust their thinking at moments of crisis. While emotion was always a part of a speculative bubble, the primary reason these occurred often came down to *misjudgements* – errors in framing the problem – rather than sheer unconsidered lunacy.

Take tulip mania. In the early 1600s the burghers of Amsterdam were in the grip of a national obsession. For a long time the Dutch had led the world in useful, practical financial innovations. The world's first stock market – the Amsterdam Stock Exchange, which opened its doors for trading in 1602 – was one such invention. The first exchange had come about because the Dutch East India Company prevented its financial partners from withdrawing their capital. Allowing them to do so jeopardised the financial certainty the company needed to plan future projects. The new stock market allowed investors to sell their financial share of the company to an investor without the change in ownership affecting the company. It was a good idea, but the tulip bubble which came a few decades later took on a crazy momentum of its own.

Speculators paid immense prices to own a tulip bulb for a few days before selling it on to an even more enthusiastic acquirer. Semper Augustus, a tulip whose flower blossomed with deep red petals and white streaks, was sold in 1625 for 2000 guilders. A few years later (in 1638), Rembrandt's *The Night Watch* was commissioned for a similar price. And 1625 was just the start. The bubble lasted all the way till 1637, only ending when a speculator who had bought a bulb at auction refused to show up and pay. Along the way tulip mania threw up all kinds of innovations. Futures contracts were traded widely. Merchants created an option to purchase a certain bulb at a certain price in the future. These contracts in turn became objects of speculation. (To the modern trader, of course, these are now standard practices.)

Tulip mania seems absurd today. Mike Dash, a British journalist, wrote in his account of the period, "It is impossible to comprehend the tulip mania without understanding just how different tulips were from every other flower known to horticulturalists in the 17th century." But it was not the distinctiveness of tulips that caused the financial mayhem. Nor was it that traders had become fixated on a bogus asset. Applying Tversky and Kahneman's work, we can see that it was something more subtle. It was the tendency to assume that the immediate past predicted the future. Once the bubble had started, what fed it was not a delusional love of tulips. It was the myopic belief that tomorrow's price would be higher than yesterday's without reference to a longer stretch of time. In other words, investors had focused on the last week of tulip prices and missed the last few decades. It was the kind of mistake they made at LTCM. And it was the kind of mistake we might all be prone to make at the roulette table.

3.

It is tempting to conclude from this and other such stories that human nature does not change. The alternative is to argue that while societies may not remember the mistakes of history, individual people do. The children of the people who had solved the Duncker candle problem weren't at an advantage when they first saw the problem. But once they had seen it, they didn't get it wrong twice. In the same way, an investor burnt by tulip mania was unlikely to have taken their cash and put it straight into another risky venture – but their descendants may have invested in a dotcom stock.

This is an important distinction. We cannot curb the human tendency to reach for the magnifying glass. There will always be moments when we choose poorly by fixating on something that doesn't matter. But even the most zealous of advocates can be turned around if they are led to consider the correct elements of the problem – that is, if they reframe the way they think about it. Take an example from the recent global financial crisis. Although much of the discussion afterwards was taken up with the question of how best to respond, the grander question was why it had happened at all. One of the more astute answers to this question was given by one of the market's great friends.

On 23 October 2008, Alan Greenspan was called to testify before a US congressional committee on the origins of the crisis. Until 2006, Greenspan had been the chairman of the Federal Reserve for almost two decades. By keeping interest rates low, he had earned a reputation for feeding the fires of economic growth and prosperity throughout the 1990s and 2000s. With credit markets now in a deep freeze and bankers feeling the chill, Greenspan was invited before the committee to give an account of himself. Greenspan's testimony to Henry Waxman, Democrat of California and the committee's chairman, was revealing:

> *Greenspan:* What I'm saying is, yes, I found a flaw. I don't know how significant or permanent it is. But I've been very distressed by that fact. But if I may, may I just answer the question –
> *Waxman:* You found a flaw in reality –

Greenspan: Flaw in the model that I perceived as the critical functioning structure that defines how the world
works, so to speak.
Waxman: In other words, you found that your view of the
world, your ideology was not right. It was not working.
Greenspan: Precisely. That's precisely the reason I was
shocked, because I had been going for forty years or more
with very considerable evidence that it was working
exceptionally well.

With these remarks Greenspan showed a certain willingness to adjust his perspective on the basis of new facts. The
flaw he had found concerned how well banks were able to
evaluate risk. One of his key assumptions had been that
self-interested organisations (and investment banks, in particular) were able to sidestep calamitous events because it
was in their own interest to do so. But what had brought
them undone in late 2007 had not been a lack of self-interest.
It had been an inability to detect risk.

In his testimony Greenspan said:

It's been my experience, having worked both as a regula-
tor for eighteen years and similar quantities in the private
sector, especially ten years at a major international bank,
that the loan officers of those institutions knew far more
about the risks involved in the people to who they lent
money than I saw even our best regulators at the Fed
capable of doing.

However, the tools these loan officers had picked up were more like magnifying glasses than mirrors. Greenspan went on:

> In recent decades, a vast risk management and pricing system has evolved, combining the best insights of mathematicians and finance experts supported by major advances in computer and communications technology. A Nobel Prize was awarded for the discovery of the pricing model that underpins much of the advance in derivatives markets. This modern risk management paradigm held sway for decades. The whole intellectual edifice, however, collapsed in the summer of last year because the data inputted into the risk management models generally *covered only the past two decades*, a period of euphoria. Had instead the models been fitted more appropriately to *historic periods of stress*, capital requirements would have been much higher and the financial world would be in far better shape today, in my judgment. (Emphasis added.)

The mistake Greenspan had identified was remarkably like the one John Meriwether and the LTCM team had made in the '90s and the biases Tversky and Kahneman had uncovered in all of us a decade before that. We tended to focus on what lay in the immediate past and miss the bigger picture. Appreciating that was the first step to solving the problem.

Greenspan did not go far enough in his critique. The problem wasn't only that bankers viewed the world through a magnifying glass. Incentives and institutions had developed to encourage them to behave that way. You could write a book (and many have) about the institutional structures which locked people into this way of thinking, largely by rewarding them with profits for decisions where they bore no personal financial risk. And whereas the bankers at LTCM may have borne the brunt of their losses, this was the exception rather than the rule. However, the point of including Greenspan's testimony here is to suggest that, after moments of defeat, readjustment may be possible.

Of course, finance is full of computer geeks and maths majors, so it's just the sort of place where you will find people who view the world through the magnifying glass of a computer model. But the lesson of reframing is transportable beyond the world of high finance. Take an entirely different problem – like war. Is it possible to fight a war and find out four years later that you have been missing your target? And if so, is the secret to winning to reframe the enemy?

CHAPTER 2

HOW TO SPOT GUERILLAS
in the mist

In March 2007 a reporter at the *Washington Post* asked David Kilcullen whether shooting Osama bin Laden was important to ending the war on terror.

"Not very," he replied. "It depends who does it." Kilcullen outlined two possible scenarios. "Scenario one is, American commandos shoot their way into some valley in Pakistan and kill bin Laden. That doesn't end the war on terror; it makes bin Laden a martyr."

The other scenario involved insurgents turning on bin Laden and executing him in accordance with their own laws. "If that happened," he said, "that would be the end of the al-Qaeda myth."

Kilcullen, who at the time was working as a senior counterinsurgency adviser to General Petraeus, the commander of the multi-national forces in Iraq, was making a subtle point about the war on terror. Winning the war wasn't about killing terrorists, he later told me. It was about tackling the insurgency that gave rise to terrorism. One of these targets was easy to see: they carried guns, flew planes and threw bombs. The other, and arguably the more important, was virtually invisible to most people, including the military.

This second way of framing the conflict was counterintuitive at first. It focused on networks, which were hard to see. The reason most people missed it – and why they zoomed in and fixed on destroying the enemy – arguably had to do with psychology. Daniel Simons and Christopher Chabris, two psychologists at Harvard University, had spotted a similar phenomenon in the way people behaved in ordinary social settings.

In 1998 the pair had conducted a social experiment in which two teams of basketball players – one wearing white shirts, the other black – passed a ball vigorously between them. The game lasted a minute, and a recording was shown to a group of Harvard students. Before viewing the video, the students were given a task. Some had to count passes by the white team; others, those by the black. At the end of the video they were asked if they had spotted anything unusual. In half the cases, the answer was no. But for the other half of the class, it was yes: they had seen someone in a gorilla suit walk into the circle of players, beat their chest and walk off. The invisible gorilla experiment won't work on you now because you know what's coming. If you want to test it, try the YouTube video on an unsuspecting friend.

The results of the invisible gorilla experiment were surprising, and soon after they were published the experiment went viral. In their paper, Simons and Chabris asked why so many people had missed the gorilla. It came down to cognition, they explained. When we *looked* at the world, we sometimes couldn't *see* some things. It was an odd thing to say, but the meaning was plain enough. By fixating on certain objects or ideas, we could be oblivious to other trends and phenomena in the world around us. The gorilla was invisible, not because it didn't exist, but because it was invisible to us. Once we were alert to our own blindness, we rarely made the same mistake twice. Participants who knew about the gorilla saw it every time.

The invisible gorilla was one example. Another was when we looked for a seat in the cinema. Often we would find the seat but miss some friends waving wildly right in front of us. The broader point of the experiment was this: how we processed information mattered greatly to the quality of our final answers. First impressions were often red herrings.

The invisible gorilla experiment seemed salient as SEAL Team Six entered bin Laden's compound on the outskirts of Abbottabad and shot the man who had held the Western world to ransom for over a decade. Would bin Laden's death end the war on terror? The answer depended on how you framed the war. If the war was about shooting the terrorists, then bin Laden's death was a killer blow. But if the correct system in focus was something less visible – people who were spurred to arms by their view of Islam and the West – then ending the war would be rather more complicated.

In the early years of the George W. Bush presidency the journalist Bob Woodward reported that the president saw the war in very concrete terms. In the top drawer of his Oval Office desk Bush kept a file on America's twenty-two most wanted terrorists – what the president, a baseball fan, called his "scorecard". Each time one was killed or captured, he put an "X" through their image. It was one way of measuring the progress of the war on terror. It focused on a highly visible target – the fighters with guns shooting at coalition forces. But it was not necessarily the most successful approach.

1.

In 1946, shortly after the Allied forces had vanquished Hitler, a French general called Raoul Salan was sent to Vietnam to conduct several interviews with Vo Nguyen Giap. Salan was on a negotiating mission to reaffirm French authority in Vietnam. The mission was ultimately unsuccessful: Giap went on to become one of North Vietnam's most celebrated generals. He defeated the French army at Dien Bien Phu in 1954 to end the First Indochina War and commanded his side to victory against the Americans more than two decades later. Giap was anti-Western, anti-modern and a communist. But in 1946 he confessed in the interview with Salan that his greatest influence in military thinking had been a Briton. "My fighting gospel is T.E. Lawrence's *Seven Pillars of Wisdom*," he told Salan. "I am never without it."

We will return to T.E. Lawrence, better known as Lawrence of Arabia, in a moment. But before we do, we should note that Giap's choice was an unusual one: most Western military planning had long been influenced by a very different thinker, Carl von Clausewitz. Clausewitz was a Prussian soldier and intellectual. In 1832, after his death, his wife published what would become his most notable work, *On War*. The book set out his principles for defining military conflict. For Clausewitz it was centrally about armies and nations. Wars were won when an army was able either to "overthrow the enemy" by force or "occupy some of his frontier-districts". Although the political dimensions of a military contest were acknowledged, they tended to stay in the background.

The Clausewitz code reflected how Western conflicts were fought from before the time of Napoleon right through to the twentieth century. By and large, warfare was organised violence between nation-states, where the final outcome was decided by the clash of armed forces on the battlefield. When generals overcame unconventional obstacles, these were largely victories of technology and battlefield tactics rather than of rethinking the nature of the enemy. The riddle of the trenches during the First World War, for example, required generals to overcome the stalemate of frontal assault by changing their tactics rather than their definition of victory.

Lawrence's contribution to military thinking was to help reframe the battlefield. In the same way that capital markets proved too complex to be captured by the financial models at Long-Term Capital Management, Lawrence argued that some military contests were too complex to be won as a clash of arms between two sides. Place the wrong system in focus and you get the wrong answer.

Lawrence didn't invent guerila warfare. Nor was he the first British soldier to write about it. In 1896, C.E. Callwell had written *Small Wars: Their Principles and Practice,* which drew on Britain's experience running an imperial police force. However, Lawrence was one of guerila warfare's most successful modern practitioners. He had arrived at his insights while serving in the Middle East around the time of the First World War. Shortly after Germany declared war on Russia, the Ottoman Empire agreed to align itself with Germany. The decision encouraged Hussein, the Sharif of Mecca, and his son Faisal, to lead the Arabs in revolt against the Ottoman Turks and reclaim much of the Middle East for themselves. The British army agreed to loan a small band of intelligence officers to the Arab tribesmen to assist in their rebellion.

The Turkish army numbered 50,000 troops, with well-defended strongholds in places like Medina. The Arabs, by contrast, had about 3000 men. Lawrence's first impression of the conflict was that the tribesmen were doomed. But he quickly realised that this was only true if he applied the conventional frame of Western military training, with its obsession that "the ethic of modern war is to seek the enemy's army, his centre of power, and destroy it in battle."

Lawrence argued instead that the most efficient way to defeat a larger enemy was to exhaust it physically and psychologically through small incursions and strategic ambush – that is, by guerilla combat. Defending against this kind of enemy was "messy and slow, like eating soup with a knife". The Arab fighter was especially well equipped to wage a freelance guerilla war. Unlike in Western-trained armies, each soldier was trained to fight for himself. "The Arab was simple and individual," he noted. "Every enrolled man served in the line of battle and was self-contained. We had no lines of communications or labour troops. The efficiency of each man was his personal efficiency."

Lawrence had led an Arab insurgency, but in the decades that followed his lesson would largely be taken up by national revolutionaries. Mao deployed insurgency tactics to come to power in China. The same methods were used by Che Guevara and Carlos Marighela in Latin America. By the time the British army turned to the Malaya Peninsula in 1948, Lawrence's tactics were being used *against* the Empire.

The Malayan Emergency was a messy battle fought between British Commonwealth forces and the Malayan National Liberation Army, the military arm of the Malayan Communist Party. Fresh from fighting combat along conventional lines, the British forces failed to spot the guerilla. Many of the Malayan army's most effective tactics did not involve a gun.

The Malayan communists had detected a high degree of disaffection among the local population with the British. By drawing the British Army into combat through jungle-based ambushes, the insurgents induced a heavy-handed response that incited further ill will. One military academic, Richard Clutterbuck, wrote that "new brigade commanders would arrive from England nostalgic for World War 2, or fresh from large-scale manoeuvres in Germany." They were equipped physically and mentally to win battles by force, and the political and social dimensions of the conflict were largely invisible to them.

A significant change to British tactics came in early 1950, when Lieutenant General Sir Harold Briggs was appointed Director of Operations. Briggs shifted the focus of the war from shooting the enemy to winning over the population. He argued that addressing local political grievances was the correct approach: it would placate the population and isolate the insurgents. His plan was later implemented under Lieutenant General Sir Gerald Templer, who took over in 1952. Templer looked beyond the visible conflict. "The shooting side of the business is only 25 per cent of the trouble and the other 75 per cent lies in getting the people of this country behind us," he later said. This was not a pacifist approach. Templer encouraged the population to provide information about insurgents by offering services like running water, medicine and electric lighting. When they were not forthcoming, fines and punishments were instituted. Templer also made use of the SAS to engage the enemy in small, targeted offensives rather than grand, sweeping battles. The shift in Templer's thinking was to fight using levers which lay beneath the surface – economic inducements, social services and the creation of stable government.

The Malayan Emergency ended with Malaysian independence. While colonial control of the country was over, the British regarded the engagement as a victory because the communist insurgency was defeated and stable government installed. Yet, despite the many publications which the Malayan Emergency spawned, the deeper lesson – the need to look at the enemy outside the traditional frame of reference – was slow to be incorporated in military thinking. The lessons of Malaya were lost in Vietnam, when the United States, now the world's leading superpower, confronted a guerilla conflict of its own.

In 1964 General William Westmoreland took over as commander of American forces in Vietnam. Westmoreland approached the war as a "search and destroy" mission to defeat the Viet Cong armies, which at the time were under Vo Nguyen Giap's command. Giap deployed Lawrence's tactics to command Vietnam's villages and attack the US army by stealth. The strategy was effective. While Westmoreland succeeded in frontal assaults, such as the engagements in Ia Drang and the Tet Offensive, he did little to win over hearts and minds.

Over time units were created to help with this. In 1965, for example, Combined Action Company units were formed to target local towns and villages. These forces blended US marines with Vietnamese national guards and built strong relationships with local communities to isolate them from the Viet Cong. These units were given greater prominence from 1968 onwards when General Creighton Abrams took over general command, but it was too little, too late. The war effort had exhausted the American public and a newly elected President Nixon ordered the withdrawal of troops.

One of the take-away messages for the United States from Vietnam was not to reframe the nature of difficult military engagements but to avoid them. Colin Powell, who later became George W. Bush's secretary of state, served as a young major in Vietnam. In 1992, Powell, as chairman of the Joint Chiefs of Staff, wrote an influential article in *Foreign Affairs* entitled "US Forces: Challenges Ahead", which helped inform military doctrine for a decade. Among other things, Powell argued that the US should not enter any foreign conflict in which the outcome of military action was not clean and clear. It would prove astonishingly successful in delivering victory in America's conventional battles, such the First Gulf War in 1990–91. But the United States couldn't always choose its battles.

2.

At the same time the Powell Doctrine was emerging in the United States, a young Australian army captain was living in the jungles of West Java and studying the elements of what would soon become the next wave of global military conflict. David Kilcullen – the man interviewed about bin Laden in the *Washington Post* in 2007 – spent the mid '90s doing fieldwork in political anthropology in Indonesia. What he uncovered would help reframe the war on terror a decade later.

Kilcullen's research concerned a separatist Muslim insurgency movement called Darul Islam. He had come across information on the group while visiting a museum in Indonesia one day. Darul Islam was virtually unknown in the West, but the group had waged an insurgency against the Indonesian government in the 1950s and '60s with a force twice what the British had faced in Malaya.

"What was interesting about the conflict was that the Indonesian government had won hands down," Kilcullen later told me. "What I wanted to know was why."

The villages Kilcullen was studying were nestled amid the 5000-foot peaks of the Priangan ranges, which had housed the insurgency half a century before. Kilcullen had been given two escorts from the provincial governor's office to look after him, but they soon got sick of the trekking around.

"They said 'Alright, well, we're going back to Badung. Give us a call if you need us and we'll come out and visit you once a week,'" Kilcullen told me.

Once they left, a subtle shift occurred in the way the locals talked to him. Until then he had been receiving predictable answers. "People were really nice and friendly and I was getting a whole set of answers associated with this previous, dead insurgency," Kilcullen said. But one evening, as he sat unaccompanied on the porch of his cabin, four young men – one carrying a case and the others long knives – slipped into the village and paid him a visit. Two of them were locals. The other two were Arabs. When they arrived, the Arabs asked Kilcullen a series of questions. Why was he interested in Darul Islam? Why had he not just gone to the library? And how many times had he come here before?

The case turned out to carry a guitar (the knives had disappeared by this point) and the youngest pulled it out, suggesting they sing some songs. The first set of questions had been relatively straightforward. But as the night wore on, the Arabs' questioning became more intense. What did he think about Israel? Did he like the United States? And why was it failing to defend Muslims in the Balkans against atrocities by Christian Serbs?

The questions struck Kilcullen as irrelevant at the time, but after that night the population around him began to open up. The answers they had given him were wrong, they said. They had a different story – the true one – which they were now willing to share.

Kilcullen, it turned out, was working amid a live insurgency. It had been dormant for decades, but the complaints that had led to its original existence had begun to reappear. "The Darul Islam guys were saying to me: 'We're still being oppressed. Our religious freedom is being abused by the Soeharto dictatorship. That's why there is still an active movement.'" But the insurgency couldn't be understood (or defeated) as a contest between two military actors charging at each other with guns. Its essence could only be grasped when you ventured further afield into something far more messy: local political grievances.

The presence of the Arabs was curious. At the same time that the Darul Islam insurgency was re-emerging in Indonesia, Al Qaeda was trying to recruit it and other local insurgencies into its developing global war. "In the year of my first research trip," Kilcullen told me, "the bigger Darul Islam movement was making a decision about whether to go with Al Qaeda and the global jihad or stick with its original separatist ambitions."

Kilcullen was learning that rather than a single foe to be engaged in well-defined, frontal combat, the global jihad was an amalgam of complex, interconnected political alliances. In this part of Indonesia, there was the local insurgency, Darul Islam. It was nativist, highly traditional, against modernisation and primarily concerned with local issues. Then there was Jemaah Islamiyah. It was a globally oriented organisation with close links to Al Qaeda. It wanted to establish a caliphate across South-East Asia and was trying to harness Darul Islam's local grievances to help fight the bigger war. The two groups were working together, but to defeat them required different approaches.

In the end the Darul Islam movement stayed local, but it changed the way Kilcullen framed the answer to terrorism. There were two kinds of terrorists, he later told me. One was the global jihadist who travelled to join the front line of conflict. These were implacable radicals who were best engaged in the heat of battle. In Iraq, for instance, Kilcullen estimated they were only 2 per cent of the enemy. The rest were local insurgents who might happily have stayed out of the battle if their grievances were addressed. Vanquishing these fighters came down to isolating them from the global jihadists and fixing the politics. The distinction was important because it showed which approach was appropriate to solving the problem. Shooting the guys with guns was not always the right answer.

Tackling local grievances was how the Indonesian government had defeated the Darul Islam insurgency in the 1950s and '60s. It was also a clue to how the modern war on terror could be won. The insight emerged gradually through the early 2000s, but in the late '90s it was not yet clear.

One salient question before 9/11 was what to make of Al Qaeda. In 1998, truck bombs had simultaneously killed people near US embassies in Kenya and Tanzania. The bombs were later connected to local members of the Egyptian Islamic Jihad, who were Al Qaeda–linked separatists. In late 2000, the US Navy destroyer USS *Cole* was bombed while it was harboured in Yemen. Al Qaeda claimed credit. The question, which Richard A. Clarke, then chair of Bush's Counter-Terrorism Security Group, posed to Secretary of State Condoleezza Rice in early 2001 was this: "Are we serious about dealing with the Al Qaeda threat? ... Is Al Qaeda a big deal?" If Al Qaeda was just a small group of implacable terrorists, Clarke said, it might be the case that the problem could never be completely eradicated – just contained. The group would be "a nuisance that killed a score of Americans every 18–24 months". But if they were part of a living, breathing organism recruiting local malcontents to wage a global campaign of terror – well, that was a different matter entirely.

Kilcullen had seen the need to reframe how we approached these conflicts. The correct system to place in focus was not the terrorists – the implacable fighters – but their networks – the global insurgency. The global insurgency was the living, breathing organism, and defeating it meant dismantling hostile social networks and severing the link between global jihadists and a warring local population.

Where would you look to find these networks? And how would you go about dismantling them? These questions were examined by Marc Sageman in his book *Understanding Terror Networks,* published in 2004. Sageman is a former CIA operative and forensic psychologist who left the organisation to research the biographies of terrorist suspects. His sample included over 400 terrorists, all of whom had already targeted the United States in some way.

By studying their histories, their relationships and how they got into terrorism, what he uncovered flipped the stereotype of a terrorist.

Sageman argued that most of the people in his sample came to political violence by what he called the "halal theory of terrorism". Most terrorists were *not* poor, rural peasants with a medieval education. Surprisingly, they were often well-educated professionals and semi-professionals with a lower-than-average bias towards mental disorder. In most cases, they had joined the global jihad through a friend or a family connection. Many, in fact, joined while living abroad, "especially in an unwelcoming non-Muslim Western country". While they may not have always had religious inclinations, their alienation from the liberal West had radicalised them. In many cases, their entry into jihad had been brokered by an agent working inside the mosque community.

Sageman's findings were enlightening because they revealed the true nature of the problem. The best methods for tackling terrorism didn't necessarily focus on what was the most visible symbol of the problem: people with turbans and guns. Instead, winning the war on terror came from disassembling the social network that connected alienated individuals with a way of "saving the world". Terrorists, Sageman concluded, were often just a group of guys patched into violence by a few last-minute encouragers sitting within a deeper network. "The suicide bombers in Spain are a perfect example," he wrote. "Seven terrorists sharing an apartment and one saying 'Tonight we're all going to go, guys.' You can't betray your friends, and so you go along. Individually, they probably would not have done it."

The information Sageman had used was all publicly available. One of the most remarkable things about the book, the CIA later admitted, was just how much insight he had gleaned from open-source material. But the system in focus for Sageman's research was largely absent from the approach the administration was taking towards terrorism around the same time. As far back as his 1999 presidential campaign speech, Bush had argued that the military needed to frame its wars in terms of clearly defined targets and highly visible actions. The US military "needs the rallying point of a defining mission ... Sending our military on vague, aimless and endless deployments is the swift solvent of morale," he said. This approach to warfare was evident as the administration prepared its entry into Iraq.

3.

Throughout 2002, the US military top brass wrestled with how to remove Saddam Hussein from power as cleanly as possible. When the moment came in 2003, they were extremely successful. Steve Metz, a national security expert at the Strategic Studies Institute, described the invasion campaign as "masterful". American forces, spearheaded by the 3rd Infantry Division, raced alongside the Euphrates River to enter Baghdad from the west, while a parallel force led by the 1st Marine Expeditionary Force attacked from the east. Within twenty-one days of major combat operations, the regime was over.

But in the months that followed the invasion, violence in Iraq grew rather than subsided. In a single twelve-hour stretch in August 2003, insurgents blew up Baghdad's chief water supply, fired rounds into one of the city's prisons and set fire to a major oil pipeline. A few days later, a car bomb was detonated near the Jordanian embassy in Baghdad, killing nineteen civilians. Donald Rumsfeld, the US secretary of defense, pinned this sort of violence to Saddam's regime. In an interview with Todd McDermott on WCBS-TV he blamed "people who were the enforcers for the Saddam Hussein regime – the Fedayeen Saddam people and the Ba'ath Party members and undoubtedly some of his security guards".

It was impossible to know who was responsible for these terrorist acts, but the point was that they were intended as propaganda rather than direct combat. Militants were wreaking havoc and encouraging the Iraqi population to blame the US military for the chaos. The real fight was a political one rather than just a clash of arms. As the violence worsened, it sparked an immune-response reaction, transforming many Iraqis' disaffection with Saddam's regime into aggression towards the US occupier. By being deaf to the political dimensions of fighting terrorism, the military had not only gone about the problem with the wrong system in focus. They had made matters worse.

Mike Shervington, a British soldier who served in Iraq, later wrote in an article for the *Small Wars Journal* that the actions of Paul Bremer in the immediate reconstruction period were particularly unhelpful. Bremer had flown into Baghdad in May 2003 to take over as Iraq's top civil administrator. In his first month of service he gave two orders. First, he disestablished the Ba'ath Party, the anti-Western political party which Saddam had led. The move was popular in some parts of the United States, but inside Iraq it created a groundswell of anger among many of those purged. Bremer needed to remove Iraq's senior leadership, but the ensuing political vacuum was exploited by insurgents.

Next, he dissolved Iraq's security forces, its army and the Republican Guard. The decision deprived 400,000 people of their jobs and salaries. Mercenaries literally wandered the streets of Baghdad as guns for hire. Shervington later summarised the situation as follows: "Overnight the political and military landscape that had been in existence in Iraq for 30 years was changed. Humiliated, angry and armed, scores of former soldiers and officers decided at that moment to form a resistance movement."

Shervington was not the only officer in Iraq capable of seeing the political dimensions of the war. Major General David Petraeus was also acutely aware of what was going on. As Petraeus led the 101st Airborne Division into the northern city of Mosul in 2003, he applied counterinsurgency tactics to reverse the conflict and placate the enemy. Petraeus filled the political vacuum in Mosul, Iraq's second-largest city, by reactivating economic activity and establishing a local bureaucracy capable of providing the community with essential services. He also initiated a reconciliation commission to administer justice for those who had been associated with Hussein's regime. Within months, Mosul became one of the most secure cities in the Iraq theatre of war.

Petraeus had not learnt to see the invisible side of war overnight. In the 1980s he had earned his doctoral degree at Princeton University with a dissertation titled "The American Military and the Lessons of Vietnam". The thesis examined the impact of the Vietnam War on America's senior military leaders. Petraeus argued that the war had a chastening effect, encouraging the military establishment to shy away from certain conflicts instead of changing the way they solved them. Many had not yet made the conceptual shift needed to embrace counterinsurgency thinking. The conclusion of Petraeus's 328-page dissertation was that this was a potentially grave mistake. A rapidly globalising world meant the United States was about to encounter more complex conflicts, including "the rise of terrorism". A new way of framing these problems was due.

Petraeus's success at Mosul led to promotion. In June 2004, a few months after his return from Iraq, he was made lieutenant general with responsibility for the Multi-National Security Transition Command in Iraq. His job was to fashion the new Iraqi Security Forces. After fifteen months he was assigned to command the Combined Arms Center, at Fort Leavenworth – the army's think-tank. It gave him an opportunity to tackle the intellectual project he had been working towards since Princeton – reframing the way the military viewed insurgency. He focused on the army's education system, ensuring that training officers made counterinsurgency a top priority before troops were sent into action. But the shift in thinking within the establishment was really enabled by a complete rewrite of the army's field manual of counterinsurgency operations.

On 10 January 2007, President Bush announced on television that he would be sending more than 20,000 additional troops to Iraq in a surge intended to end the war. A few weeks later Petraeus was appointed Commanding General of coalition forces in Iraq. The extra troops were needed because counterinsurgency was a people-intensive way of waging war. It required troops to enter a village then stay there to build relationships and secure the population, rather than firing a few rounds and moving on.

The Bush–Petraeus Surge in 2007 proved devastatingly effective in quelling the conflict in Iraq. In September 2008, the Pulitzer Prize–winning journalist Steve Coll wrote in the *New Yorker* that "the statistics about reductions of violence in Iraq are irrefutable". Colin Kahl, an Iraq expert and Obama adviser, agreed. "There has been significant and meaningful improvement in the security situation since the Surge began," he wrote. "US and Iraqi forces have made great strides against [Al Qaeda in Iraq] and the organization's fortunes are likely to decline further."

Key to Petraeus's success was his idea to target the connections *between* the insurgents rather than the insurgents themselves. One of the most important moments in the surge was the decision by Sunni tribal sheikhs to realign themselves with the United States and away from the

Al Qaeda–affiliated militants. This decision by the Sunni leadership, known as the Anbar Awakening, had not been of Petraeus's making. The Sunnis had eventually become tired of Al Qaeda's brutality, its religious puritanism and globalist ambitions. Petraeus's skill, though, was to recognise that this divergence was important and exploit it for all it was worth.

The US military began to treat local Sunni fighters as allies rather than opponents, a kind of local "coalition of the willing". They also began to offer political assistance to local leaders trying to re-establish their position in the community, while at the same time playing dumb to the non-tribal Iraqis who were suspicious of this. These political networks were important to rebuilding the social infrastructure of the country. Focusing on these kinds of answers was a far more successful approach to solving the problem than the search-and-destroy tactics that had come before. "Anbar, you could just feel it flipping," Petraeus later told Steve Coll. "Really, the early spring, the mid-spring of 2007, it just started to speed down the chain."

The Iraq conflict was just one corner of the global war on terror, but it offered a template for defusing the wider situation. When you looked further afield to the theatres of Pakistan and Afghanistan, the principles were the same, but the way they applied to the facts was different. David Kilcullen, who left Petraeus's command after the Surge to advise NATO on the Afghanistan conflict, thought that only about 3000 to 4000 fighters (about 10 per cent of the Taliban forces) were hard-core global jihadists, and only a quarter of the Taliban forces were full-time soldiers. The remainder he labelled part-time fighters, often driven to the fight by local politics.

Kilcullen's analysis of the war on terror portrayed a military establishment slowly coming to terms with the hidden side of combat: "The military going in, I would argue, bounded the problem as 'How do we defeat a particular armed group in Iraq and Afghanistan?'" he told me. "They focused on the military actor – the guy with the weapon actually shooting at coalition forces. They acted as if the problem was the insurgent fighters. But the problem wasn't the insurgent fighters, it was the insurgency. It was the bigger dynamic. They had the wrong system in focus initially in terms of trying to solve the problem." Now, he said, counterinsurgency had entered mainstream thinking.

War and finance were very different issues, yet we struggled with them for the same reason. We focused on what was most visible and missed the bigger picture. The war on terror was far from over, but by reframing the conflict the military was finding a way to unlock the problem. War and finance shared something else in common. They were both affected by globalisation, the spread of ideas, money and people around the world. Globalisation was an unsettling experience. Western values were suddenly broadcast into quiet towns on the Middle Eastern frontier; capital flowed in vast sums into tiny island economies. We tended to react to the complexity of a fast-moving world by over-simplifying. In this way, war and finance also shared a space with one of the biggest political headaches of the 2000s: immigration.

The movement of people between countries was as old as human civilisation. However, globalisation was changing the speed and ease with which it was happening. Part of this was technological. Planes flew people in and out of countries more cheaply and frequently than ever before. But it also came down to growing inequality between rich and poor. Where the rich world sat next to the poor world, people tended to move across borders in a fairly predictable direction.

Immigration was deeply complicated because its contours could not be easily generalised. Nevertheless, many essential aspects of the political debate were on display at one of the world's longest rich–poor borders: that between the United States and Mexico. Many Americans saw the immigration debate in terms of its most visible feature: border security. Every day Mexicans were crossing the fence under the cover of night. This was a sure way to get people angry, but was border security the real problem behind the immigration issue?

CHAPTER 3

CROSSING THE BORDER

into Tea Party America

Robert N. Krentz Jr was more famous dead than alive. The Arizonan rancher had been found shot in the front of his all-terrain vehicle on 27 March 2010. He had gone missing shortly after radioing to his brother that he was helping someone he thought was an illegal immigrant. When the police found him a few hours later, his guns were untouched in the back and his dog had been shot and critically wounded. Fresh tracks led from the car to the Mexican border twenty miles away. The suspect was never found, but the story went national.

Krentz's death mobilised the country's anti-immigration lobby. The news confirmed their belief that immigration had got out of hand: the border zone was out of control and US nationals were losing their lives. A month after the murder, the Republican governor of Arizona, Jan Brewer, signed the toughest anti-immigration law in recent US history. It gave police the power to detain those without documentation, and citizens could sue an agency for not fully enforcing federal law. "We cannot stand idly by as drop houses, kidnappings and violence compromise our quality of life," Brewer declared, moments before putting pen to paper.

"Robert Krentz really is the face behind the violence at the US–Mexico border," Gabrielle Giffords, Democrat of Arizona, said in May later that year. At a press conference announcing an additional 1200 National Guards to the border, Giffords held up a photograph of Krentz. But there was another side to the story, which was picked up by the *New York Times*. Krentz may have been the face of the violence, but the rate of violent crime along the border (and across Arizona) had been declining. Further, if it was indeed true that Krentz's death was connected with drug smuggling, then it would have been the first such killing in almost three decades. When the *New York Times* checked this with Sheriff Larry A. Dever of Cochise County, he confirmed it was true.

The Krentz murder highlighted why immigration was such a diabolical political issue in the United States. It was true that drug-related crime was a problem along the border. Mexican cartels had been trafficking illicit substances through the country's south-west for decades. But as a piece of the puzzle it was relatively small. For a start, the White House had bipartisan support to tackle drugs and improve border security. No one condoned the drug trade or encouraged entrants to break the law. Yet immigration provoked such raw emotions in spite of this agreement because the heart of the problem remained largely unaddressed.

Border security was an easy way to frame the immigration debate because it was visually compelling. Throughout the 2000s, news channels broadcast images nightly of Mexicans crossing into America. To anyone who saw the footage, the solution to the immigration problem was obvious. The president had to call in the National Guard to patrol the border and build taller fences. One man who had made this connection more forcefully than most was a Republican congressman from Colorado, Tom Tancredo. Days after Krentz's death, Tancredo flew to the border to draw attention to the issue. "We should demand from the President of the United States that we put the National Guard on that border," he told followers in a video posted on his website. "The Governor of the State of Arizona should do that immediately."

Tancredo was a man who didn't mince words, but there was evidence to suggest he was missing the point. Calling in the National Guard would change nothing. Both sides of Congress wanted to stop illegal immigrants. The challenges they faced in doing so were mainly technical. Smugglers were always inventing new ways to transport drugs. In one case a medieval-style catapult had been used to sling them over the fence. In another smugglers had used well-placed spotters to guide human mules via text message. By pointing the magnifying glass at the border, Tancredo encouraged people to miss the bigger picture. There *was* a problem with immigration in America, but to frame it correctly you had to look well inside the country.

1.

On 8 September 2010, Senator John McCain of Arizona – who ran against Barack Obama for the American presidency – travelled to Sandoval, New Mexico, to speak on immigration to the Southwestern Border Sheriffs' Coalition. The coalition had been formed in 2007 to coordinate the law-enforcement efforts of twenty-six counties along the border. As McCain delivered his speech, he focused on everything about the issue that you could *visualise* was wrong.

"Ten years ago, we could not have anticipated the headlines that routinely appear in newspapers today throughout the country," McCain told his audience. For example, the 2 September headline in the *Arizona Republic* read, "Mexico: Soldiers kill 25 in shootout near border." The 31 May headline in the *Dallas Morning News* warned residents that "Incidents on the Texas Border Lake Raise Fear of Spillover Violence From Mexico." Every day the Tucson sector, inside Arizona, alone apprehended between 700 and 1200 illegal border crossers.

The US–Mexico border, McCain concluded, was horribly porous. In a speech earlier that year he had defended the passage of Arizona's new law. The "unsecured border between Arizona and Mexico ... has led to violence, the worst I have ever seen," he told the US Senate. He went on to cite numbers for illegal immigrants "that stagger".

The journalist William Finnegan, writing for the *New Yorker*, said McCain was right: the numbers were indeed staggering, but not in the way he meant. Apprehensions of illegals were sharply *down* over the decade. The Department of Homeland Security had kept statistics on Border Patrol apprehensions between 2000 and 2009. Across the country, about 600,000 people had been stopped in 2009, down almost 300 per cent on the number in 2000 (1.8 million). The decline was even more pronounced along the south-western border, where the number had declined from 1.6 million to 540,000 over the decade.

You might think the fall in apprehensions reinforced why border security was a problem – perhaps more illegals were getting past authorities undetected. That conclusion seemed unlikely. At the same time apprehensions had dropped, federal funding in border security had gone up. The number of Border Patrol agents on the south-western border had doubled in the six years to 2010. The region had also constructed more than 600 miles of fencing. Everything suggested that the number of illegal immigrants entering America was dropping. Ronald Vitiello, the deputy chief of US Border Patrol, said as much in his testimony to the House Committee on Homeland Security in May 2011. "While our work is not done, every key metric shows that these collaborative border security efforts are producing significant results – in fact, studies and statistics have shown that some of the safest cities and communities in America are along the border."

How could McCain's speech about the parlous state of the border be reconciled with reality? The answer seemed to be this: while violence along the border was generally falling, a few spectacular stories had grabbed the headlines.

Dramatic events tended to distort people's perception of reality, making border security seem like a bigger problem than it actually was. Krentz's murder by what most people assumed was a drug smuggler was one such example. "There is nothing more powerful than a story about a gruesome murder or assault that leads in the local news and drives public opinion that it is not safe anywhere," said Scott Decker, a criminologist at Arizona State University, shortly after the murder. "Hard as it is to change the crime rate, it may be more difficult to change public perceptions," he added.

The less charitable view was that McCain was whipping up public opinion by zooming in on a shiny object. The irony was that McCain, more than most, knew how difficult it was to calm the public when this connection was made. In 2007 he had almost lost the Republican primary vote for appearing soft on border security compared with his rivals. As he toured the country, his opponents Mitt Romney and Rudy Giuliani switched tack and geared their campaigns towards "Tancredo-ism" – the new national pastime of inspecting the border with a pair of binoculars. All sorts of popular fears could be projected onto border crossers.

"Am I a terrorist?" a professor had asked McCain sarcastically during one of his primary speeches. It caught McCain unawares and he was momentarily speechless. "With those sneakers, you're not a snappy dresser," he said. "That doesn't mean you're a terrorist. Though you terrorise the senses." McCain's awkwardness epitomised why the country broke down into seething aggression over the issue. There was nothing about immigration that you could solve working from first impressions.

The magnifying glass itself had been fixed in place by an international catastrophe. Before 9/11, lobbyists on both sides of the political divide had worked with Washington to bring into view immigration's economic dimensions. After the terrorist attacks they watched in shock, then sadness, as the nation shrunk its focus. At a conference held several months afterwards Demetrios Papademetriou, a prominent immigration campaigner, told an audience that there was now only one way to address the issue. "Take everything you ever wanted for immigration reform before 9/11 and put it in an envelope clearly marked SECURITY," he said.

The failure of politicians to defuse the immigration bomb did not come down to a traditional left–right debate. President Bush, for example – a pro-immigration Republican – was no great fan of Tom Tancredo. In the week before September 11 he had welcomed Vicente Fox, the President of Mexico, to his Oval Office garden and promised to legalise hundreds of his countrymen then living within US borders. After the 9/11 attacks, however, the deal was off.

2.

Bush, to his credit, made several attempts to pass comprehensive immigration reform during his two terms as president. One explanation for why he failed was that he framed the problem in the wrong way. By hanging the reforms on two issues in particular – the status of Mexican guest workers and border security – he missed some of the deeper emotions propelling the issue: the economic pain registering in the American heartland. Two commentators who made this point were Ross Douthat from the *New York Times* and Reihan Salam from the New America Foundation. Douthat and Salam were a new breed of conservative – bright, young and impeccably educated. In their book *Grand New Party*, they argued that the Republican Party was forgetting its working-class roots. To defuse the immigration issue, you actually had to solve a different problem. You had to bring back jobs and economic prosperity to America's working class.

Since the 1970s and '80s, America's conservative party had become increasingly radical, they argued. It had moved away from its base and pursued ideological causes. Sunny-side free-market radicalism was one example of this. By zealously promoting an abstract idea the party had become distinctly non-conservative. "There have been moments where a 'government is the problem' argument has resonated with working-class Americans," they wrote. But this unrestrained optimism, for the most part, glossed over "the persistent unpopularity of the [Republicans'] small government message."

Immigration was one area in which Republicans were fighting the wrong battles. While they had animated people's fears about illegal immigrants, they had not relieved their pain. The legal/illegal distinction was a technically legitimate one – it excited lawyers and retired military personnel.

However, it was not the real problem. The real problem was much harder to see. "Globalisation and the rise of the knowledge-based economy, growing outsourcing and the demise of lifetime employment ... have left American workers feeling more insecure," Douthat and Salam stated. All these things were hurting low-paid workers and those looking for work. The flow of cheap labour from Mexico was causing brutal competition for jobs.

To be sure, there were economic benefits from low-skilled migrant labour. For one, it helped the rich get ahead. It enabled affordable nannies, low-cost restaurant services, cheaper retail shopping and a well-priced house cleaner. But these were the jobs which poorly educated Americans had long vied for. As illegal, low-skilled Mexicans began to flood the labour market, these Americans were finding themselves out in the cold. You couldn't solve the problem by just shutting the border – you would still have the problem of low-skilled workers coming to America legally. But complaining about a Mexican's legal status was the polite way of phrasing things. Beneath the surface lay the indignity of unemployment.

Douthat and Salam had fired their shot at the conservative elite. However, there was evidence to suggest that their message had cross-party appeal. One ally was Paul Krugman, who had won the 2008 Nobel Prize in Economics and was a well-known progressive. In 2007 Krugman had conceded in the *New York Times* that the economic dimensions of the immigration puzzle deserved more attention. "I'm instinctively, emotionally pro-immigration," he told his readers. "But a review of serious, nonpartisan research reveals some uncomfortable facts about the economics of modern immigration, and immigration from Mexico in particular."

The uncomfortable facts stemmed from the work of one of America's leading labour economists, George Borjas. Borjas had discovered a link between increased Mexican immigration and the wages of the poorest Americans. The popular myth had been that Mexican workers filled a vacuum in the economy: that they did, as President George W. Bush once put it, the "jobs that Americans will not do". Krugman's conclusion was that this was "intellectually dishonest". When the supply of labour went up, basic economics said wages went down.

Borjas's most authoritative study was co-authored with Lawrence Katz, a former chief economist for the US Department of Labor. The pair had taken census data stretching back to 1900 and studied the correlation between demographic changes and wages. Borjas and Katz noted that Mexican immigration had not always been a problem. It was only in the '70s and '80s that Mexicans had started crossing into America in droves. Before then, most of America's immigrants had come from across the Atlantic. As the Mexican economy began to tank, the source of the inflows changed. At first the effects were small. In the border state of Texas, only 1.9 per cent of the workforce was Mexican in 1970. By 2000 it was nearly 11 per cent.

Race, of course, did not explain why Mexican immigration affected wages. It had to do with levels of skill and education. In general, skilled migrants were an economic plus. No one much complained when a foreigner came to America and worked in a university or Silicon Valley. Skilled migrants contributed more than they eventually received. The tension arose when migrants had fewer skills than the average population. And by the 1980s, Mexicans were arriving with substantially fewer skills than the average American. The new flood of Mexicans spurred a price war in which low-paid Americans were hurt the most.

Krugman put the problem as follows. First, the net benefits to the US economy from immigration were small. "Realistic estimates suggest that immigration since 1980 has raised the total income of native-born Americans by no more than a fraction of one per cent," he wrote. Second, while immigration raised overall income slightly, it hurt poor Americans. The Americans worse off were those whose jobs required little education – waiters, retail employees, labourers and so on. Third, low-skilled immigration put pressure on the social safety net. "Unfortunately, low-skill immigrants don't pay enough taxes to cover the cost of the benefits they receive," Krugman wrote.

Of course, immigration helped the individual Mexican workers immensely, a point which Krugman's friends thought he should have focused on. But it was the effect on the native-born American labour force which really troubled him. "Immigration is an intensely painful topic for a liberal like myself, because it places basic principles in conflict," he concluded. "But it's important to be intellectually honest, even when it hurts."

Some academics disputed Borjas's findings. One of the most prominent was the Canadian David Card, whose best-known study was of an episode called the Mariel boat-lift. In 1980 a group of 125,000 Cubans had been transplanted to South Florida after Castro allowed an exodus, and about half of those had settled around Miami. The effect was that the city's population grew by 7 per cent over just a few months. The episode was what economists called "an event study", a unique event which allowed them to study effects in isolation. When they compared developments with those in other cities, they could see the relative effect.

Card compared the economy of Miami with those of four cities – Tampa, Atlanta, Houston and Los Angeles – over the period 1980 to 1987. The conclusion was that immigration did nothing to weaken the economy. True, crime rose as career criminals entered the new population. There was also severe social anxiety as the local population reacted badly to the changes. But what didn't change were the wages of the poorest workers. In fact, compared with the other cities in the study they even rose slightly. "The Mariel influx appears to have had virtually no effect on the wages or unemployment rates of less-skilled workers," Card wrote.

Card's study faced various challenges. The main one came from Borjas himself, who argued that a city-based study distorted the economic effects. In such a study, there was no way of accounting for the possibility that low-skilled native-born workers just packed up and left. This would have a neutralising effect on wages in that city. The local influx of labour would no longer be so severe. Across the entire economy, however, the net effects of the immigration would still be acute. This was the main distinction between Card's and Borjas's work. Whereas Card studied cities, Borjas studied macroeconomic effects.

The exact economics of immigration could be examined in ever greater detail. But the political point was this: the economic side of the problem had been left out of the picture. Law enforcement was a seductive way to frame the immigration debate because it was easy to broadcast pictures of Border Patrol officers on the nightly news. Whether it allowed you to solve the problem, however, was far from clear.

3.

In 2008 the United States elected its first black president. It was an event so remarkable that it was said to herald a new era in America's attitudes to race. But as the new president forged ahead with a legislative agenda to regulate the finance and health sectors, he faced a backlash which threatened his success. Supporters of the president said the backlash came from racial fear and hate. To capture its essence, however, one had to home in on something more complex.

The face of the presidential backlash was the Tea Party movement. Its emergence was slow and disorganised. The tipping point came when Rick Santelli, a banker and cable news reporter, stood on the floor of the Chicago Mercantile Exchange in February 2009 and denounced the government's plans to insure householders defaulting on their mortgage repayments. "We're thinking of having a Chicago Tea Party in July," Santelli said as traders cheered in the background. "All you capitalists that want to show up to Lake Michigan, I'm gonna start organising." Within two years, the Tea Party had become the fastest-growing political movement in America.

Santelli's role as catalyst for the Tea Party was ironic. Most members of the movement were not wealthy bankers or downtown office types. They were older, lower middle-class Americans – ordinary Republican voters – often made jobless by the financial crisis. They were also mainly white. Their former workplaces were the empty car factories of Detroit and the abandoned coalmines of Colorado. Many were new to organised politics. What tied them together were falling house prices and record rates of unemployment. "I think the Tea Party was an idea ... started by some pissed-off Americans that are sick and tired of being forced into things," said one recruit who had been retrenched from the General Motors factory in Ohio.

The Tea Party railed against what it saw as high-taxing, imperial government in Washington that had failed to look after its interests. But big government was only part of the story. A related source of anger was the question of immigration. Theda Skocpol and Vanessa Williams, two political scientists from Harvard, had made this point in their book *The Tea Party and the Remaking of Republican Conservatism*. While "defence and spending" usually ranked first among Tea Partiers' most important issues, "border security and immigration" came in a close second. The Tea

Party epitomised how lingering tensions over immigration and jobs could be fused into a potent political force.

In his documentary *Tea Party America*, the British journalist Andrew Neil showed footage which made this point. Neil had travelled on a bus to Washington DC to join Glenn Beck's rally "to restore honor". Along the way he spoke with Mario from the Kentucky Tea Party. Mario was a "birther", someone who questioned whether Obama was in fact born in the United States. As they sat on the bus together, their conversation took a strange turn.

"I'd *seriously* like to see that birth certificate. I'd like to know where my president was born and whether or not he is a citizen," Mario said.

"But we've seen the certificate," Neil interjected.

"Ah, no we haven't. We have seen a reasonable facsimile of it that is not valid and not legal," Mario replied.

"You don't seriously believe he's not an American?"

"I don't know, I don't know," Mario said, shaking his head.

The bus to Washington carried messages written on its side. "Go back wherever you came from Obama," read one. "Go back to Kenya," another. In public, Obama had denied that race played a part in the opposition to his presidency. In private he held a different view. In May 2010, Obama had told a private White House dinner that race was the "subterranean agenda" of the Tea Party's opposition.

What were we to make of the Tea Party movement? Many were clearly decent, hard-working people who had found themselves on the underside of capitalism. Some Tea

Partiers were antagonistic towards foreigners, but only a minority seemed to be racist. In one instance a Bostonian Tea Partier had been kicked out for a racial slur he had posted on a website. "This country is made up of people from all countries, that's what made us what we are. I wouldn't want it any other way," another member responded. To explain the hostile sentiment toward immigration and foreigners, you had to look to the state of the economy.

As early as the 1960s, psychologists had shown that opponents of immigration were not always racists. When you peeled away the hostility, it was often independent of race. More important than whether someone was black or Latino was how they fared in the competition for economic resources. Psychologists called this the "in-group" and "out-group" mentality. The in-group were those who were part of the native-born population, and the out-group were the fresh arrivals. When times were good, immigration wasn't an issue. When times were tough, people's attitudes towards the out-group reached their nadir. People blamed recently arrived, low-skilled migrants when it meant their own livelihoods were under threat.

You could see the same thing happening in Europe and beyond. As the European Union had expanded its reach in the 2000s, workers in impoverished Eastern Europe had packed up their lives and caught the next train west. The flow of economic migrants into the rich parts of Europe caused immense social unrest. However, this was usually seen as a country-specific problem. In France, President Sarkozy called on all cop-killers of immigrant origin to be stripped of their citizenship. In Britain, Prime Minister Gordon Brown was reduced to making a grovelling apology on his 2010 election trail after he dismissed Gillian Duffy, a life-long Labour voter, as a bigot for her concern about the number of immigrants from Eastern Europe. In the Netherlands, reputedly Europe's most tolerant country, the problem was the same. Lilianne Ploumen, chairwoman of the Dutch Labour Party, acknowledged the "loss and estrangement" that Dutch people felt in the face of Turkish migration to their country. "The street is mine, too. I don't want to walk away if they're standing in my path," she told the electorate.

The immigration problem was extremely complicated, taking a different form in each country. However, beneath all these different manifestations was a consistent theme: the tension caused by a modern global economy. In the 1980s and '90s, goods and capital markets had been opened up to international trade. By the 2000s, the same was happening to labour markets – to people. As globalisation increased the mobility of low-skilled workers, job security came severely under threat.

4.

Immigration was a political issue which didn't have an obvious end point. It was hard to imagine how you might reverse the flow of people across borders or solve once and for all the competition for resources. What did that mean for our ability to solve complex problems? To answer that question we must extend our understanding of how such problems work.

So far in this book I have assumed you can eliminate complex problems. Now I have to inject some modesty into that assumption. Actually, complex problems are not like maths puzzles. You cannot always reframe them, see the answer, and have the problem disappear. It is possible for a problem to change its dimensions over time and reappear in another complex form. The idea that problems are constantly evolving redefines what we mean by a solution. Solutions do not necessarily end the conversation; rather, they return the debate to a steady and stable state. To appreciate this point we need some history.

In 1989, the political scientist Francis Fukuyama wrote an influential essay in which he argued that history was coming to an end. "In watching the flow of events over the past decade or so, it is hard to avoid the feeling that something very fundamental has happened in world history," he wrote. Fukuyama was referring to the end of communism. The Cold War had shaped foreign affairs since the end of the Second World War, and as the wall dividing East and West Berlin was torn down, Fukuyama pronounced the last great struggle of political ideas over.

Fukuyama extended his essay into a book, *The End of History and the Last Man,* published in 1992. It was not the first time someone had declared history to have come to an end. The German philosopher Georg Hegel had made a similar prediction a couple of centuries earlier. Hegel's ideas had come to prominence in the salons of Paris in the 1930s, when the Russian emigré Alexandre Kojève lectured on Hegel at the prestigious École Pratique des Hautes Études. Hegel picked 1806 as the end of history. The date was significant because Napoleon defeated the Prussian monarchy in the Battle of Jena that year. Once Napoleon trounced Europe, Hegel argued in *The Phenomenology of Mind*, the continent was imbued with the ideals of Enlightenment France. At the same time these ideals travelled east to fan the flames of the revolution in America.

Liberty and equality had been the victors of history, according to Hegel. Those two principles were the terminus of man's struggle with his fellow man. Now most problems were administrative in nature. Certainly, some reforms were still needed to implement these principles. There was a need to abolish slavery, extend the vote to workers and minorities, and give women equal rights. But the really big ideological contests – the battles of ideas – were over. Henceforth the world's problems would be rather ordinary.

According to Fukuyama, Hegel had been more or less right. His prediction had just come two centuries early. The twentieth century had seen two profound assaults on Western liberalism. First Hitler had waged war in defence of fascism. Then the Soviet Union had pursued socialism with its own brand of vigour. Both of these political movements had their own versions of how history would end. Marx, for example, co-opted Hegel to promote his own favoured ending: revolutionary struggle overthrowing society's class divisions. The problem for Hitler and Marx was that fascism and socialism had both lost. With economic and political liberalism now ascendant, the world's problem-solvers could go into retirement. For Fukuyama there was even a kind of sorrow in this. "The willingness to risk one's life for a purely abstract goal, the ideological struggle that called forth daring, courage, imagination and idealism ... will be replaced by economic calculation, the endless solving of technical problems, environmental concerns, and the satisfaction of sophisticated consumer demands," he wrote.

Fukuyama was right in a sense. Some problems had ended with the fall of the Berlin Wall. It was true that the world was no longer divided between liberalism and socialism. But there was still residual anger at liberalism: implacable terrorists were driven by deep hostility towards the West. And it was true that people were more or less reconciled to the triumph of capitalism over communism. But there were still tensions: the ability of bankers to pool money like poker chips gave most people heartburn.

The world no longer wrestled with clear-cut contests of ideas. We were not going to unwind Western civilisation at the behest of a few terrorists or roll back capitalism because of near-sighted bankers. Nevertheless, solving the new kind of problem was diabolically tricky. We weren't fighting over grand, abstract goals, but to argue that what was left was merely "technical" underestimated the complexity of this newly fashioned world.

To be more specific: Fukuyama's thesis implied that the world's biggest problems had discrete *endings*. It was a heroic view of history. Problems were solved like medieval jousting contests where two knights – equally radical and opposite in their beliefs – charged at each other, with only one victor. This view of history had a very particular interpretation of "solving" a problem. A problem was only *solved* when one of the possible two answers was vanquished. Solutions were traded in right and wrong, good and evil, with no room in between. "In the post-historical period there will be neither art nor philosophy," Fukuyama had said, "just the perpetual caretaking of the museum of human history."

An alternative view of history argued that society had become more complex since 1989, not less. The new kind of problem – the one which saw the shades of grey – demanded an alternative kind of solution. In 1973 two academics from Berkeley, California, Horst Rittel and Melvin Webber, had foreshadowed this in their article "Dilemmas in a General Theory of Planning". Rittel and Webber labelled these problems "wicked".

Society was made up of many different domains, said Rittel and Webber. Each was connected with the others like limbs on a body. Imagine, for example, that the media was one such limb. What happened inside the media had kick-on effects for government. That interaction was one degree of wickedness. The government in turn influenced the economy. This layer was a second degree of wickedness. It was the connection between these different domains that made a problem wicked.

Problem wickedness was just a way of describing society's complexity. Society was an organic thing, constantly changing and adapting. This was not a new idea. The British statesman Edmund Burke had said a similar thing in the late eighteenth century. But Rittel and Webber argued that globalisation was increasing the degrees of wickedness in social problems. We were becoming more networked and connected than in previous epochs. In a simpler age, people had assumed that the world was becoming more homogenous. With the victory over fascism, for example, people had said in the 1950s that society would soon share the same values and beliefs. With the end of communism, Fukuyama had made a similar prediction. Globalisation, however, produced a world which was more various, not less.

In a globally connected world, what it meant to "solve" a problem was very different from Fukuyama's conception. It was hard to *end* problems in this kind of environment. The best you could hope for with a wicked problem was that the problem would be contained. "Wicked problems have no stopping rule," Rittel and Webber wrote. Solutions were measured by different units of analysis – better or worse, stable or unstable.

5.

So far in *Reframe* we have examined complex problems at one level of wickedness. In finance, we examined the clash between mathematics and money. In terrorism, it was the battle between the military and politics. In immigration, it was between law enforcement and the economy. The next problem we will consider with at least three degrees of wickedness. It will take us across the many domains of society – from the media to science to technology.

Climate change is not a new problem. It is the continuation of problems that are actually quite ancient. What makes it special is the way it connects many domains within society: this is what makes it such a wicked problem. Inspect any one domain and the mistakes we make are the same as those which entangled us in our finance, war and immigration problems. Add them together and you get a particularly messy challenge.

CHAPTER 4

MEDIA MAGNATES

and intellectual magnets

When Kumi Naidoo took over as the head of Greenpeace International in December 2009, he talked about climate change as if it had to do with carbon emissions. When we met six months later on a train travelling from Oxford to London, the conversation had changed to a chat about the weather. Targets and timelines equalled glazed eyes, he explained. Stories about the weather were far better for grabbing people's attention.

In 2007 Kumi had walked through transit at London's Heathrow Airport and spotted the front page of the *Independent* newspaper. It carried a picture of an animal skeleton lying in the empty bed of the Murray River. Above it a caption read, "Is Australia the first rich country to experience climate change?" Just that visual, Kumi said, leaning forward intently, was more powerful than the thousand-word article inside.

I had met Kumi after a speech he gave at Rhodes House in Oxford in 2010. Kumi was a legend among Rhodes scholars, and by any measure an extraordinarily impressive man. On the day he had been awarded his scholarship in Cape Town in 1986, he had called up his father to share the good news. He was told not to return home. The police had taken his brother and were looking for him as well.

The police wanted Kumi because he was a zealous anti-apartheid activist. As a fifteen-year-old he had been expelled from school for campaigning against racial inequality in the education system. Around the same time, his mother committed suicide. "She just reached a moment where it felt too much," he told a reporter in 2009. Kumi home-schooled himself, entered university and became active in Durban's political underground.

A few years later, on the night he discovered the police were after him, he fled the country and started making his way to Oxford. Shortly before crossing the border he visited his closest friend and ally, Lenny Naidu. Lenny had been a man way ahead of his time, Kumi told me. He had been one of South Africa's best philosophers, political thinkers and activists. As they finished a cigarette together, Lenny asked Kumi a question.

"Kumi," he asked, "what is the greatest thing you can do for the cause of freedom?"

Kumi paused. "Well," he said, "I suppose it would be to give your life."

"Wrong," Lenny replied. "It is not to give your life. It is to give the rest of your life."

Two years after this, Kumi was called to a friend's room in Magdalen College to take a phone call from South Africa. Lenny and some of Kumi's other friends had attended a rally in Cape Town and been shot by the police. Lenny's body had so many bullet holes in it that his parents couldn't identify him. Kumi was reminded of their last conversation and made a lifelong commitment then and there to a career in activism. Kumi ended his speech in Oxford with the story, which gives you a sense of how small I felt when, two hours later, I found myself sitting opposite him on the 7 p.m. First Great Western service to London.

Our meeting got off to a slow start. I mumbled my way through a summary of my doctoral research and explained why I was keen to talk to him. I was interested in the politics of climate change, and curious to know why he thought people struggled with the issue. He began with a few general statements, but then, when he realised I was an Australian, switched to the topic of the Murray-Darling River Basin.

The drought in the Murray was something I knew a bit about. The river had been reduced to a trickle for over a decade and water politics was high on the agenda back home. Newspapers were filled with stories of farmers forced to pack up their lives and sell their farms to the bank.

Kumi argued that the drought showed the effects of climate change. But as he made the connection between the Murray-Darling Basin and what needed to be done to promote climate policy, I grew uneasy. The connection between the drought and climate change was not entirely clear to me. Australia had always had droughts, and the Murray-Darling drought had broken sometime in 2008. Was it true that the drought was caused by climate change? If so, once the drought broke, was climate change over?

I put this question to Kumi as we trundled through Reading Station. He answered by switching to a different example from a place he knew better: Africa. About a year beforehand, the former secretary-general of the United Nations, Kofi Annan, had released a report by the Global Humanitarian Forum. The report tallied deaths from climate change to date. The Atlantic Ocean was swallowing coastal villages in West Africa. The drought in Lake Chad had turned tribes in Central Africa against each other. Kumi paused to let the stories sink in. "We can already say that 300,000 people have died *from* climate change today," he said.

As the words left his mouth, my back stiffened. Disputing the cause of death of 300,000 people was no way to make friends, but the truth was I struggled with what he was saying. Lake Chad had been in drought since the 1960s, well before the world's population had doubled and carbon emissions had skyrocketed. As for sea-level rise, parts of the world had been inundated by the ocean for millennia. How did Kumi know which events were connected with climate change and which were long-run, naturally occurring weather events? Our conversation carried on in this fashion until we reached Paddington Station: Kumi's events, my doubts. When we arrived, we were both exhausted.

"All the best with the research," Kumi said with some effort as we reached the gates. "I'm sure it will be great."

On the train back that night I tried to figure out why Kumi and I were so different. I admired the man. Since leaving Oxford he had waged wars against dictators, pulled people out of poverty, tackled AIDS in Africa and fought apartheid alongside Nelson Mandela. My achievements were microscopic by comparison. Yet his way of seeing the world baffled me. I was not a climate sceptic. My doctorate at Oxford was, after all, in the economics of climate change. But Kumi had an irresistible impulse to put a face on something which was virtually impossible to see.

In one respect, of course, Kumi was right. Showing a picture of a man standing up to his waist in floodwater warmed up the crowd. But in another respect, he was using the wrong tools to fight his fight. His argument was entirely reversible. He could point to the drought in Africa, but a sceptic could just as well point to lush farmlands in Europe to make the opposite case. You could say a spate of unseasonably hot days in 2006 showed the effects of global warming, but you could just as well pull the file out on 1906, 1806, 1706 – right back to the Jurassic.

The weather was something you could see and feel on a daily basis. It was a compelling way of framing the problem because it fitted nicely on a television screen. There was just one problem with it: climate change wasn't about the weather, it was about the climate; and changes in climate were barely perceptible over a decade. If you wanted to examine climatic *processes* rather than weather *events*, you needed to have a different system in focus. Kumi Naidoo was a seasoned political strategist. It wasn't hard to work out why weather events were easier to campaign on. But you didn't need to be a political genius either to work out that the strategy would backfire.

1.

Kumi's approach to converting sceptics was what I called the finger-licking approach. It assumed that people could lick their finger, point it in the air and say with confidence, "Yep, I think the average annual temperature *has* risen about 0.3 degrees Fahrenheit over the decade." Having made this assumption, winning the political argument was about stuffing the airwaves with many more such weather events to point the finger at.

Kumi was relatively new to environmentalism when he was appointed executive director of Greenpeace. When he went to his first day of work, two weeks before the UN climate change conference in Copenhagen in 2009, he had never worked for an environmental organisation before in his life. He was the first outsider to head Greenpeace, but you could see why they would want to hire him all the same. What Kumi lacked in green credentials, he more than made up for in charisma and storytelling ability. Kumi was extremely good at telling dramatic stories.

The realisation that climate change activism needed more stories came to Kumi at Copenhagen. He had spent his first two weeks on the job cramming statistics on carbon emissions and targets. When the media came hunting, he regurgitated them with precision. His about-turn came after his brother, who had been watching his media appearances, gave him a call to offer some advice. Since being released from prison his brother had become a professor in optometry in Durban. "All that talk about degrees and percentages and

350 parts per million, Kumi, and you had me lost," he said. "You forgot the first rule of political campaigning. It's all about images."

If Kumi's brother was right, the trick to winning over public opinion was simple. More graphic stories on climate change would mean more support. But the problem with this conclusion was that history contradicted it. Over the twentieth century, news stories on climate change had steadily grown in number. The first such story was published by the *New York Times* in 1932, when a staff reporter covered the melting of the polar ice caps. The story lay dormant for the next five decades but was picked up again in the 1980s, as human-caused climate change received more research funding. The screening of Al Gore's *An Inconvenient Truth* had pushed awareness of the issue to historic highs in 2006. Then there was a lull before the build-up to the Copenhagen conference in 2009. Although the issue had lost steam since then, the long-term upward trend in coverage was clear.

It was not only that people were receiving more information about the changing climate; they were also hunting down more information. Google kept data on terms plugged into its search engines. They showed that interest in stories on "global warming" and "climate change" had matched the upward supply of news stories. As people read more stories about climate change, they also became firmer in their beliefs. In the United States, one of the country's leading pollsters, Gallup, had tracked how well people felt they understood the issue for over two decades. In 1992, 53 per cent of Americans said they understood climate change fairly well or very well. By 2008 the percentage was 80 per cent. The pattern was replicated across most of the developed world.

Awareness was one thing, concern was another. In 1988, the United Nations had created the Intergovernmental Panel on Climate Change. The IPCC was a body charged with the task of surveying the academic literature and providing the world with a summary of the state of scientific opinion. In the four assessment reports it published – 1990 (updated in 1992), 1995, 2001, 2007 – its researchers gradually became more sure of their findings. But over the same period the concern of ordinary voters stayed flat. In the United States, one of the world's best-informed democracies, about the same number of Americans worried "a great deal" about climate change in 2008 as they had done in 1990. In Britain and Australia the numbers were similar.

The state of climate politics could be described by the following formula. We were being fed more stories about climate change. We were absorbing more stories about climate change. But our assessment of the danger of climate change was steady.

One conclusion to draw from this might be that stories did not change public opinion. We could choose the weather as our system in focus, but weather events oscillated so frequently that the effect was neutral over time. This conclusion was correct over the long term, which was why Kumi's strategy was ultimately flawed. But over the short term it was true that people responded to stories and anecdotes. People were happy to draw big conclusions from a sample size of one. When there were droughts and hot weather, public concern was up. When there was snow and flooding, public concern was down. People's reactions to weather events were volatile over the short term. Over the long term, however, public concern stayed flat.

Here is one example of just how fickle people could be. As luck would have it, the pollsters Populus asked several thousand people in Great Britain the same question in November 2009 and in February 2010, a mere four months later. Nothing had changed in mainstream scientific opinion over Christmas, but a number of sensational events had hit the evening news.

The first was an incident involving scientists at the British University of East Anglia. In what was dubbed the "Climategate" scandal, hackers uncovered emails suggesting that the researchers had doctored contributions to the IPCC report of 2007. When the allegations surfaced, searches for the terms "climate change emails" and "climate change hoax" on Google soared.

The second was the conference in Copenhagen. It had been hyped up by the media as the "Treaty of Versailles for climate change". When it ended, it was largely reported as a diplomatic failure.

The third story, which was indirectly related to these but more potent, was Europe's coldest winter on record. Holiday flights were cancelled as blizzards shut down the continent, and families were able to walk on their local estuaries for the first time in a generation.

The impact of these events was to violently shift public opinion. Between November and February, the BBC revealed that the number of people who thought climate change was "an established fact" had dropped from a half to a third of those surveyed. Those who thought climate change was not happening grew from 10 per cent to a quarter. Those who still "believed" but thought climate change had been exaggerated rose (up 14 per cent) to cover just over a third of those surveyed.

Gradual changes of opinion are normal in political polling. Wild swings are rare. When the BBC tried to explain the wild swings, they found that one (or all) of the three items caused people's blood to boil. People were flipping over these stories. Their impact corresponded with how graphic an image they evoked. Most people had heard about the leaked emails (57 per cent), but the debacle at Copenhagen rated higher (61 per cent). The most powerful story of all was the weather. Eighty-three per cent of those interviewed knew that Europe had just experienced its coldest winter on record. People formed their opinions by reacting to events.

The polls coincided with Kumi's first four months with Greenpeace. His reaction to the polling figures was to provide counter-stories. It was a natural reaction. It was exactly what had happened in climate politics for as long as anyone could remember. The mistake was to assume that the only reason people struggled with climate change was that they could not visualise it. But visualisation *was* the problem. People bounded a problem by focusing on the symbols and missing the deeper causes. In terrorism, the military had seen the insurgents but missed the insurgency. In financial markets, traders had seen the last five years of data but missed the last five decades. Climate change was a different issue, but the problem was the same. People focused on what they saw out the window and injected a larger meaning into it. They saw the weather, but the climate was invisible.

In May 2010, 255 members of the US National Academy of Sciences made this point in an open letter published in newspapers around the globe. "There is nothing remotely identified in the recent events," they explained, "that changes the fundamental conclusions about climate change." If Kumi was going to devise a political strategy that changed public opinion over the long haul, he needed to do something very different.

2.

So far in this chapter we have talked about the political strategy of one of the world's biggest environmental groups. But an environmental group is just the kind of organisation which might be forgiven strong rhetoric in getting its message across. To appreciate why climate change had become so badly stuck as an issue by 2010, you had to realise that it was more than just Greenpeace pointing out the window. Ironically, the group best at deploying Kumi's political strategy were his opponents, climate sceptics. The difference was that they focused on the opposite kind of weather event: global cooling.

On the evening of 18 December 2009, a private jet with "United States of America" emblazoned on its fuselage rose from Copenhagen airport and headed west. It carried a man who had staked his political legacy on climate change. In his 2008 nomination victory speech in St Paul, Minnesota, Barack Obama had told the American public that he wanted change on two things in particular: health care and climate action. "Energy we have to deal with today," he had said in a debate against his Republican opponent, John McCain. "Health care is priority No. 2."

Eighteen months later, though, the US president was flying into a snowstorm. All along the country's eastern seaboard, towns and cities languished in snow. Washington DC, where Democrats and Republicans were negotiating a congressional bill for him to tackle his signature issue, had disappeared under twenty inches of it. You didn't have to be an Obama supporter to appreciate what the president's media strategists were up against. Building momentum on global warming was a nightmare when the magnifying glass was pointing in the wrong direction.

When Obama made his commitment in 2008, it was a good year to go hard on climate change. Hurricane Katrina had ripped its way through the American heartland just a few years earlier. John Holdren, a Harvard professor who would go on to be President Obama's science adviser, told a reporter at the *Guardian* that year that Katrina was turning people around on global warming. "Overwhelmingly the public has been convinced not just by theoretical arguments," he said, "but their experience of the climate changing around them and what they are watching on their televisions." But of course that positive sentiment could easily be reversed when things changed.

After returning from Copenhagen, the Obama administration attempted to regain momentum on its flagship issue. On 9 February 2010, it announced that it was setting up a federal agency to study the effects of global warming on society. The news sent the country's shock-jocks into delirium. Rush Limbaugh, the voice of one of America's most popular radio programs, said that the snowstorms were a "nail in the coffin" for climate change. It was "absurd", he told his audience, that Obama would consider setting up a federal department on climate change "amidst record-setting cold weather".

Gretchen Carlson, host of Fox News's *Fox & Friends*, said that the proposed department and the snowstorms were a "dichotomy". Carlson's co-host, Steve Doocy, agreed. Ordinary folk didn't need scientists to tell them what to think. All they had to do was look out the window. "It's interesting, given the fact that the weather is so rotten right now," he mused on morning television. "People are asking, 'How can there be global warming if it's snowing and it's fairly cold?'" The editor of the *Washington Times* chimed in. "Snowmageddon," he wrote, was "undermining the case for global warming one flake at a time."

To anyone who had spent a few years in climate change circles, it was just another round in the inevitable to-and-fro. In his Christmas reflections of the year before, Christopher Booker, the British climate sceptic and journalist, had said something similar. His *Telegraph* article read, "2008 was the year man-made global-warming was disproved." Booker's argument was clear to anyone who could read a date and a headline. On 21 May 2008, the *Telegraph* had published an article titled "Climate change threat to Alpine ski resorts." On 19 December, the same paper ran another article titled "The Alps have best snow conditions in a generation." How were these two weather conditions – hot and cold – able to coexist? So long as the world experienced record cold temperatures, Booker slammed global warming as a myth.

Christopher Booker and Kumi Naidoo may have sat at different ends of the political spectrum, but they had this in common: they used the same strategy to draw the crowds. They both rode the tide of events. Their political instincts taught them to feed human biases rather than resist them. The strategy involved flicking new stories under the lens of the magnifying glass. It was an exhausting way to do combat.

The point was not lost on political insiders in the United States in 2010. In February, a reporter asked Senator Jeff Bingaman, a Democrat from New Mexico, about the prospects of a congressional bill on climate change passing, given the snowstorms. His response summed up the magnifying glass trap perfectly. "People see the world around them and they extrapolate," he remarked. But by April that year, who was winning the climate change debate had become moot. A much more visual environmental issue had seized the political agenda. British Petroleum had leaked black, stinking oil through the Gulf of Mexico.

3.

Where did all this talk about the weather leave us? When climate change was framed as a debate about the weather, the issue could be spun indefinitely. For a while the sceptics would win with the snowstorms in the United States. Then the believers might triumph with the heatwaves in Europe. The tide would then turn in Australia, as the north-east of the country was drenched in a downpour. The vintage years for believers were 2007 and 2008, while 2009 and 2010 were better for sceptics. But in the long run, the weather epitomised political stalemate. It was a never-ending story.

Another version of seeing weather as climate change was when advocates argued that weather *volatility* signalled climate change. Weather volatility did not change the system in focus. We were no better at deciphering climatic change from fluctuations in weather than we were at remembering that period of heatwaves/snowstorms when it looked like our side was winning. No one was able to measure changes in the climate with the naked eye. To pretend you could was to miss the reason why climate change struggled to gain traction as a political issue.

Any political strategy which followed the oscillation in public sentiment rather than trying to lead it was ultimately doomed to failure. The weather was the perennial news story, the best way to overcome social awkwardness and fill silences in tearoom chat. It wasn't going to disappear, nor would it lead to any long-standing political victory. It was the wrong way to frame the problem.

The alternative was to change the system in focus. Instead of arguing about the weather, we should argue about carbon. This wasn't an easy argument to resolve either, but at least it was the right one. For a start, both sceptics and their opponents acknowledged that carbon emissions were radically increasing.

In 2007 Bjorn Lomborg had published a controversial book called *Cool It*, which made the "sceptical" case against climate change action. Lomborg had made a name for himself in the 1990s as a critic of the environmental movement. However, in *Cool It* he accepted one thing without question. The world was filling up with carbon emissions. "The problem," he wrote, "is that man has increased especially the quantity of CO_2 in the atmosphere." This was not a minority view in the sceptics' camp. Nigel Lawson, Margaret Thatcher's former chancellor of the exchequer (and father of celebrity chef Nigella Lawson), thought the same thing. Lawson had retired from politics in 1989 and since made a name for himself as a leading British climate sceptic. In 2008 he wrote *An Appeal to Reason: A Cool Look at Global Warming*, which made much the same point as Lomborg had: "There is no doubt that ever since the Industrial Revolution in the latter part of the nineteenth century, man has added greatly to atmospheric concentrations of carbon dioxide by burning carbon – first in the form of coal, and subsequently in the form of oil and gas, too."

The acknowledgement that carbon emissions were growing was an important place to start if we were to resolve the political train wreck over climate change. There were, of course, those hardcore radicals who would dispute even this fact, but they were largely fringe dwellers. The growth in carbon emissions was a discernible fact in the same way that a thermometer measured the temperature: ice cores plucked from the earth's surface showed that the concentration of carbon in the atmosphere had dramatically increased. What was in dispute – and where the political argument needed to go – was what these emissions actually meant, and what to do about it. Were carbon emissions *causing* climate change, or was climate change happening anyway, or was it not happening at all? Kumi and Booker were not the right people to ask about this.

The complexity of climate change was such that even when the problem was reframed in this way, it was just the beginning. That was what made climate change such a wicked problem. It was a political shapeshifter. You could unlock one aspect of the puzzle and realise that you immediately faced another.

This crystallised for me in one of the interviews that took me to Oxford University. In 2006, the year that Al Gore's *An Inconvenient Truth* became a box-office hit, I sat before a scholarship committee in Sydney seeking their endorsement. Most of the questions they asked had little to do with my research (they wanted to know what I thought of female circumcision and whether we should outlaw boxing!). The one relevant question they did ask me was this: what happens if the theory of climate change turns out to be wrong?

The answer I gave them was that they would be wasting their money and I would have wasted my time. The truth was, I wasn't a scientist. I didn't know the first thing about building a multi-variant regression model of temperature rise or conducting climate-sensitivity analysis. But that wasn't the real issue. The real question which needed answering – and the one on which I did have a view – was this: whose expert opinion was worth listening to? And answering this was not as easy as listening to the person with the loudest voice or the scariest pictures.

CHAPTER 5

FREEDOM FIGHTERS
in lab coats

In the mid 2000s, a new craze was sweeping America's evangelical congregations. Some of the most devout, anti-environmentalist Christians were having Climate Conversions. You could walk into a church on a Sunday and find parish members kneeling at the altar and renouncing their scepticism. The phenomenon was welcomed by those arguing for action on climate change, but it raised intriguing questions: who were these evangelicals listening to, and on what authority did they accept their word?

The short answer was that American evangelicals were turning to Richard Cizik. Cizik was a stalwart Republican and the vice president of government affairs at the National Association of Evangelicals, where he had been a member since the early 1980s. The NAE is one of America's largest Christian organisations. It represents 45,000 congregations across the heartland of America and Cizik's job was to lobby Washington so that their views were heard. In the 1980s and 1990s Cizik had worked with the Bush and Clinton administrations to oppose abortion and gay marriage and do more to tackle human trafficking and global poverty. On the issue of climate change, however, Cizik had been reluctant to take a stand.

With no training in science, Cizik's impression was that scientific opinion on climate change was divided. "One side says this, the other side says that. There's no reason to get involved," he once told a reporter. And putting the science to one side, there was another reason for Cizik not to get involved. Politically speaking, climate change was a dangerous issue for a good Republican to support.

American evangelicals made up 40 per cent of the Republican base, which meant they also had a tendency to be climate sceptics. There was no obvious reason why the two things went together. Conservatives had demonstrated an enviable reputation for protecting the environment, especially in the area of conservation. Ronald Reagan, for example, had been a great protector of America's national parks. But there was something about climate change which sent many Republicans running for the sceptics' camp. If Cizik was smart, he would steer well clear of the issue.

The problem, though, was personal faith. Something shifted for Cizik in 2002 which compelled him to act. That year he was invited to attend a forum on climate change at Oxford convened by the British evangelical and scientist Sir John Houghton. Houghton was a retired professor of atmospheric physics who had made significant contributions to the findings of the IPCC. The forum he had helped organise, which lasted three days, walked a number of evangelical leaders through climate science and related it to their biblical responsibility.

In the 1960s, Lynn Townsend White Jr, an American historian, had accused Christianity of responsibility for the world's environmental degradation. In an article titled "The Historical Roots of Our Ecologic Crisis", White had pointed to a key passage from Genesis which he said encouraged Christians to exploit the Earth: "God blessed them and said to them, 'Be fruitful and increase in number; fill the earth and subdue it. Rule over the fish of the sea and the birds of the air and over every living creature that moves on the ground.'" The passage had stung the conscience of many of the devout.

Sir John Houghton now argued that Christian leaders needed to follow a different theological principle than that of "subduing the earth". God had created the planet and it was Christians' responsibility to look after it. Failure to do so was an abrogation of their duty. It was not good enough to dismiss climate change as God's will.

Houghton's alternative interpretation of scripture, with its talk of "creation care" and "neighbour care", shook Cizik to the core. On their final day in Oxford, Houghton walked the group of evangelical leaders through Blenheim Palace, the ancestral home of Winston Churchill. That afternoon Houghton pulled Cizik aside. "Richard," he said, "if God has convinced you of the reality of the science and the Scriptures on the subject, you must speak out."

Cizik's immediate response was to sit tight. Supporting climate change was bound to have ramifications for his career, as well as for the amount of funding the NAE could attract. These were good reasons to do nothing. But then, after reading more books and flying over a drought-stricken Africa a few months later, he decided to act.

Over the next five years Cizik built an alliance of evangelical leaders to convert Christians across America into climate change believers. In 2003 Jim Ball from the Evangelical Environmental Network had driven a hybrid car through America's Bible Belt as part of the "What Would Jesus Drive?" campaign. He soon joined Cizik. In 2004 Cizik and Ball issued a statement, "For the Health of the Nation". Released under the NAE banner, the statement laid out a rough theological basis for "Creation Care" on climate change. It evolved into the Sandy Cove Covenant of 2004 and then the Evangelical Climate Initiative, which was launched in 2006. By the end of that year, Cizik's coalition of converts included some of America's most politically and theologically conservative Christians. One was the televangelist and voice of the American Christian Right, Pat Robertson. In a radio broadcast on *The 700 Club* in 2006, Robertson confessed that he had "not been one who believed in the global warming", but that he had now become "a convert" to the cause of climate action.

The flurry of climate conversions in the American Bible Belt eventually petered out, but along the way it had revealed something important about how conviction on climate change was spread. This was best expressed by the Australian commentator Waleed Aly in his 2010 essay *What's Right?* "Let us admit up-front the most obvious, but resolutely denied, fact of the climate change debate," he wrote. "It is not, for many of its participants, about science at all." Climate change, Aly argued, was an ideological debate for many people and not a scientific one. By ideological he meant that it came down to *whom* you believed, not *what* they said. It didn't matter much whether you were a "believer" or a "sceptic". What mattered was whom you trusted.

Cizik's personal journey illustrated Aly's point. Houghton had not told Cizik anything he could not have read in an IPCC report, but what had changed was who was saying it. In Cizik's case the message was clearest when it came from scripture. Other people had their talking head of choice. American sceptics listened to Glenn Beck, the former Fox News Channel host. British believers favoured George Monbiot, the *Guardian* journalist.

What was distinctive about Beck, Monbiot and the Bible was that none of these sources was a climate scientist. Journalists were increasingly performing the role of commentator rather than news reporter. Each had authority of one kind or another, but it was not scientific authority.

The ardour with which some climate converts had seized on the issue led sceptics to joke that it had become a new religion. But the joke cut both ways. Sceptics could be just as fanatical. Climate change conviction had everything to do with whose authority you chose to accept.

1.

As evening fell on 31 December 999 AD, history records that a party of Christians ascended Mount Zion to meet their Maker. The Biblical Apocrypha had prophesied that the end of the world would arrive a thousand years after the Last Judgement. Calculating this date from the birth of Jesus

Christ, early Christians decided that the apocalypse would arrive on the first day of the new millennium. Many of the Christians who travelled from Europe had given away their worldly possessions before making the journey to Jerusalem. Their actions had not been entirely irrational. Since the world was expected to end, charity would improve their prospects in the next life. When 1 January arrived with little change, many of these people were devastated. Not only did they return to their homelands paupers. They had lost faith in the only explanation of the world that they possessed.

The point of the story was not that medieval Christians were stupid. Rather, it was that they had been too credulous. Armed with the knowledge that the world was ending, they had done exactly what was rational. Their error had been to believe that the Bible, which had great authority on religious matters, had the same authority in the physical sciences.

The question of authority in matters of Science versus Spirit came to something of a head in the sixteenth and seventeenth centuries during the scientific revolution. According to the Old Testament, the Earth sat stationary at the centre of the universe. All planetary motions were explained by orbit around it. The theory, known as Ptolemaic astronomy, had been developed in ancient Greece and was surprisingly good at predicting planetary motion. By the early seventeenth century, however, astronomical tools had improved to such an extent that astronomers began to observe that Ptolemaic predictions of planetary motion were not strictly accurate. Tycho Brahe, Galileo and others realised that if assumptions were changed so that the Earth in fact rotated around the Sun, the calculations yielded much better results.

But the claim that the Earth rotated around the Sun, known as heliocentrism, was a deeply heretical notion. Nicolaus Copernicus had published the theory in a manuscript called *De revolutionibus orbium coelestium*, which he released shortly before his death. The work was later scorned by both the Catholic Church and Protestant reformers, and the most aggressive criticism was targeted not at Copernicus's mathematics but at his authority to make such claims. Martin Luther, the German theologian, belittled Copernicus as the "fool astronomer" in one of his 1539 *Table Talks*. The sentiment was echoed decades later from the pulpit of Santa Maria Novella in Florence on 20 December 1614. Copernican thinking, preached Tommaso Caccini, was "philosophically foolish and absurd and expressly heretical". Although Copernicus had made a fine mathematician and astronomer, the Church concluded that he had been "less able in the physical sciences and dialectic, and inexperienced in Scripture".

The claim of heliocentrism was a pregnant moment in the history of scientific authority for one very simple reason. It wasn't just a theory. The claim of the Catholic Church, which had hitherto been the world's authority on all celestial matters, turned out to be empirically incorrect. The realisation that the Church was holding the wrong hand on this issue did not come suddenly. It was drawn out over three centuries of excommunication and martyrdom. The task of testing and retesting theories until their validity was established gave rise to an age of reason and helped lay the stepping stones that led to the Enlightenment. One achievement of this period was to show that something other than religious dogma offered authoritative statements on the physical world. Reason, rather than pure faith, was the tool with which nature's mysteries could be unravelled.

"Scientist" is the word we now use to describe people like Galileo. These were people who used experiments and human reason to decipher what we could not see. The idea was so new that in seventeenth-century Europe the word "science" did not exist. Scientists were simply known as philosophers about nature: natural philosophers. As for a community of scientists who worked in a profession to solve difficult problems: that was unheard of.

In letters written in 1646 and 1647 to his learned colleagues, the British natural philosopher Robert Boyle described the creation of an extraordinary new body of men enrolled in something called an "Invisible College". The Invisible College was a network of gentlemen with common interests. They included the architect Christopher Wren; Robert Hooke, who would uncover the laws of elasticity; and John Wallis, a mathematician who would contribute to the invention of calculus, to name just a few. Their aim was to share novel and experimental ideas and offer constructive criticism of each other's work. Through this loose network of scrutiny and competition, the Invisible College aspired to increase the rigour of the ideas its members produced.

In 1660, the Invisible College was formalised by King Charles II as the Royal Society of London for the Improvement of Natural Knowledge. The Royal Society grew into one of the foremost scientific institutions of its time, fostering discoveries of immense significance across the entire field of the natural sciences. Its mission built on that of the Invisible College. It aimed to promote "physico-mathematico experiential learning". Even more important than its purpose, though, was the Royal Society's articulation of something called the scientific method.

The scientific method was the semi-formal set of rules by which a theory or hypothesis could be supported or refuted by experimental evidence. For a statement to be scientifically authoritative, it needed to stand up to the critical scrutiny of other scientists. Truth, the Royal Society Fellows argued, was forged in the fire of scepticism. The Society's motto was *nullius in verba*: "Take no man's word for it." Through scepticism, experiment and debate, the Royal Society imagined a community in which objective knowledge might be attained.

It was a heady period in human history. The scientific method enabled people with sharp minds and clean sets of data to develop explanatory theories about the world. But there was a limitation to this new enterprise. Although science and scientists were capable of making reliable claims about the physical world, this did not give them the same authority to decide how society should be governed. There was a clear distinction between science and politics. If science and politics were mixed together, the authority of each discipline might be diluted.

This division of authority between science and affairs of state was an important achievement of the scientific revolution. The Elizabethan lawyer and essayist Francis Bacon had once argued that the world was written in two books, Nature and the Scriptures. The scientific profession did not need to undermine the Church's authority when it came to society. Both had their place. The Royal Society's founding statute recognised both goals: "to the glory of God the Creator and the advantage of the human race". Even Darwin, who would uncover the theory of natural selection as a Fellow of the Royal Society two centuries later, believed that his research did not provide grounds for atheism. He once wrote on the subject of religion that "the whole subject is too profound for the human intellect. A dog might as well speculate on the mind of Newton. Let each man hope and believe what he can."

But there was a third book being written at this time which Bacon had not mentioned. It was called Democracy. Democracy was the story of citizens deciding how they would be governed, independent of the Church and science. The seventeenth and eighteenth centuries had helped loosen the grip of unelected monarchs on society. In 1642, just sixteen years after Bacon's death, England was thrown into its first of several civil wars which arguably pushed the country towards greater parliamentary representation. Thinkers such as John Locke, and later John Stuart Mill, all argued in one way or another for greater faith in the ability of ordinary people to make reasoned decisions about how society should be organised.

Democracy's great virtue was that it valued the views of the many. Its danger was that an ignorant public might "insolently scorn law and reason". These were the words of the Marquis d'Argenson, a French nobleman ruling in the court of Louis XV shortly before the French Revolution. D'Argenson's fear was that certain matters were so technically complex that only an elite few had real authority over them. If a clear separation of powers was not maintained between Nature, Scripture and Democracy, then society risked a tyranny of the masses – mob rule.

The outcome of this, in France and elsewhere in Europe, was representative democracy. It was a compromise between direct democracy, where people had all of the power, and absolute monarchy, where they had none. In a representative democracy, d'Argenson wrote, "one acts through deputies, who are authorised by election; the mission of those elected by the people and the authority that such officials carry constitute the public power." Representative democracy was a significant invention because it struck a balance between the three different types of authority. It also stood for a new set of challenges. With the rise of democracy and science throughout the twentieth century, a new battleground for worldly authority had been set.

2.

The reason why we have veered into the story of democracy is that democracy is a complicating factor in what we do with science. Although only an elite few scientists are qualified to make authoritative statements about what is happening in the world, what we do with that information is up to us. The blurring of science with politics, however, has been one of the great unarticulated controversies of the late twentieth century and beyond.

The problem is a simple one. Scientists have unparalleled authority to speak on the conclusions of their experiments. However, this does not give them equal authority over the laws that should be enacted as a result of their findings. Separating out the two things is the first step to unlocking the climate conundrum. So long as climate change is framed as a choice between belief and scepticism, it cannot be solved. Few of us have the scientific skills to adjudicate on this. To resolve the debate, we must first reframe it. We must differentiate between areas of relative authority.

In 1962, the British polymath Michael Polyani wrote an article called "The Republic of Science", in which he noted something distinctive about the scientific method. "The authority of scientific opinion remains essentially mutual," he wrote. "It is established *between* scientists, not above them." To make his point, Polyani borrowed an image from the economist Adam Smith. Polyani argued that the scientific method was coordinated by an invisible hand. Instead of conducting transactions in money, science is held in check by "peer review". Peer review was the practice of withholding academic research from publication until it had been scrutinised by other expert scientists and given the tick of approval. Scientists, Polyani argued, could be trusted to be independently minded and naturally curious. As a result, their assessment of a colleague's work would not be tainted by commercial gain or vested interest.

The occasion for Polyani writing the "The Republic of Science" was that he feared scientific independence was under siege. In a previous era, scientific endeavour had been a private practice funded through philanthropy and individual means. This had allowed science to flourish: research targeted at fundamental inquiries about the physical world. But by 1962, the vast bulk of scientific funding came from the government. The public funding of science was a good thing in many respects – accountability brought greater scrutiny – but it also had a downside. "He who pays the piper calls the tune," wrote Michael Reagan in *Science and the Federal Patron*. Public accountability forced scientists to have a keener eye for how they sold their work to the public or, more specifically, public administrators.

The tension between politics and science was evident in a report published by Vannevar Bush after the Second World War. Bush was one of America's foremost educators and administrators. In 1944 President Roosevelt, soon to leave office, commissioned him to write a report which would justify the government's funding of science. The war effort had injected large amounts of money into scientific endeavour, but with the war over, Roosevelt realised it needed a new justification to keep it going. For "the improvement of the national health, the creation of new enterprises bringing new jobs, and the betterment of the national standard of living," Roosevelt had suggested in his letter to Bush.

Bush's report, *Science – The Endless Frontier,* responded by identifying two types of science. One was applied science: science that tied in closely with the vital interests of government. The other was fundamental science: science done without public goals in mind. Bush acknowledged that science had become a "vital interest" to government. Health, wellbeing and security were all areas of public policy where science had a role. But he also argued that scientists should not be too distracted from the job of doing science. They were experts in managing experiments, not voters.

Perhaps Bush's separation between politics and science was a fiction. Bush, after all, was heavily embroiled in both camps himself. During the war he had directed the Office of Scientific Research and Development and sat on the committee which advised the president on the atomic bomb. But there was another way of reading his report. It was as a plea from a man wrestling with the two directions in which science could go. Bush respected the public role of science in a healthy democracy, but he was also attached to a world where science and politics were separated by Enlightenment ideals.

In the decades that followed, science arguably moved more in the first direction than the second. Scientists still acted as Francis Bacon's "merchants of light", but now they had to venture through jungles of regulation. Their day jobs were partly bench work and partly filling out forms and writing long essays. Every major decision had to be reviewed by a board and, increasingly, public interest groups.

It started in 1946. The passage of the Administrative Procedures Act required US federal agencies to consult the public before enacting new regulations. It grew through the 1960s and 1970s. The 1969 National Environmental Policy Act, for example, required very extensive public input into all aspects of the scientific process. The National Research Council, one of the top US science bodies, was another organisation whose approach to science changed. Sheila Jasanoff, a professor in the politics of science at Harvard, has identified 1983 and 1996 as important years because they bookended an important shift in the way science was done. According to Jasanoff, the 1983 report focused on "integrity" in scientific processes, which meant scientific findings should be "separated as far as possible from the political and value-laden task of risk management". However, the 1996 report focused on scientific "accountability" – science "requiring repeated public consultation even in the production and assessment of scientific knowledge".

In other words, science was shifting from a profession ordered by the invisible hand to one governed by the public review panel. This was a departure from the ideals of the Invisible College. It also implied that public consultation improved the quality and acceptability of expert scientific judgements. "Science today," wrote Sheila Jasanoff in *Science* in 2010, "has to meet a series of public expectations, not only about its product but also about its processes and purposes." The division between science and politics was becoming blurred.

3.

All this is relevant to understanding why the issue of climate change had become so stuck in the mud by the late 2000s. In 2009, the head of the Intergovernmental Panel on Climate Change, Raj Pachauri, had stood before an audience in Abu Dhabi to deliver a speech. There is no more room for doubt on the science of climate change, he declared to a hall of world leaders and leading business figures. Those who doubted climate change were the modern-day equivalent of the Flat Earth Society. Coming from a man who purported to represent the scientific profession, these remarks were extraordinary. When a member of the audience stood up to say that scientific endeavour was premised on the notion of doubt, Pachauri shook his head. Climate science was certain and there was no wiggle room.

Raj Pachauri epitomised a new brand of politicised science. In what capacity had Pachauri made his comment that there was "no room for doubt"? If he was speaking as a scientist, he had set the bar impossibly high. But Pachauri's authority as a climate scientist was limited. He had trained as an engineer but spent his career inside bureaucracies. The more likely scenario was that Pachauri was speaking as a politician. But who were his constituents and to whom was he accountable?

Pachauri's actions created deep confusion about what the IPCC – the world's leading scientific body on climate change – was meant to stand for. Was Pachauri in charge of a scientific institution or a political one? The murkiness was not all

Pachauri's fault. Some of it had to do with the way the IPCC had been set up.

As research into climate change had grown through the 1970s and '80s, the international community called for a new worldwide body. In 1988, the World Meteorological Organization and the United Nations teamed up to approve the creation of the IPCC. The IPCC's task was intended to be purely technical and not at all to prescribe policy. World leaders needed a window onto the intellectual output of the most authoritative climate scientists. The IPCC's reports were to be published every five years and would distil what was happening in the Republic of Science into a single, easy-to-read document. The IPCC would not be a scientific laboratory but more like a publishing house. It was a giant filter, synthesising and summarising the scientific enterprise on climate change.

The tension within the IPCC was captured in its title. It was "intergovernmental". At its head sat a bureau of selected governmental representatives, not a body of independent scientists, such as the Invisible College had been. Whether or not the end justified the means, the perception was that the IPCC's work would be serving the needs of government and policy. When Lord Monckton, the British climate sceptic, colourfully decried a "world government" on climate change under the auspices of the United Nations, this may have been his point.

In practice, the giant filter which had been placed over the world's scientific community did a very good job. There was not too much distortion between the IPCC reports and independent scientific opinion. The vast majority of scientists had concluded, with growing conviction between 1988 and 2007, that man-made carbon emissions as well as natural processes were contributing to climate change. This conclusion was by no means certain. The degree of probability was said to be 90 per cent or greater.

To communicate this message clearly without oversimplifying it was always going to be difficult. Scientists hated broad strokes and sweeping generalisations. For this reason, it was hardly surprising that the first attacks on the IPCC's authority came from scientists.

Mike Hulme in his book *Why We Disagree About Climate Change* gives an example of a revolt from the late 2000s. Virtually all climate scientists agreed that climate change would cause the Greenland ice cap to melt over the twenty-first century. This process was expected to accelerate over time. As the ice melted, water would flow over the ice cap, compounding the rate of melting. Scientists understood this phenomenon in principle, but modelling it using a computer was difficult. As a result, the fourth IPCC report stated that "the understanding of these effects is too limited to assess their likelihood or to give a best estimate". The wording deeply disappointed some scientists. If people wanted to be fully informed about climate change, they argued, they needed to know about accelerated melting.

Blows were also landed on the IPCC from the sceptics' camp. In 2006, ExxonMobil, one of the world's leading oil conglomerates, claimed in its annual report that the IPCC had been overly selective in the research it was letting through its filter. The report stated that the IPCC relied on "'expert judgement' rather than objective, reproducible statistical methods". It was therefore uncertain how much warming came from carbon emissions and how much from natural causes.

Given what we know about peer review and the Invisible College, ExxonMobil's accusations were mischievous at the very least. Expert, peer-reviewed judgement *was* the method by which scientists reached objective, reproducible truths. By suggesting the two were different, ExxonMobil was driving a wedge in the public imagination between expert advice and subjective opinion. The error was so egregious that the great bastion of Enlightenment science, the Royal Society itself, decided to defend the profession. It accused the company of deception in a letter dated 4 September 2006. In this instance ExxonMobil later clarified the matter, stating that "even with many uncertainties, the risk that greenhouse gas emissions may have serious impacts justifies taking action". The correction, however, made less of a splash in the tabloids than the original statement.

The most damaging attack on the authority of the IPCC came in late 2009. In November of that year, more than a thousand emails and documents were hacked from the Climate Research Unit at the University of East Anglia in Norwich, England and posted on the internet. The emails sparked allegations about the quality of research being used by the IPCC. In one case, Professor Phil Jones, who headed the East Anglia research group, had poorly annotated a graph used in the 2007 IPCC report. Global temperatures were usually recorded using the width of tree rings, but Jones's samples did not match direct temperature recordings from the 1960s onwards. Jones and his collaborator, Michael Mann of Pennsylvania State University, had combined data from the tree rings and direct temperature recordings in order to construct the graph. They did not explicitly acknowledge this in the published tables.

After these things were revealed, a number of inquiries were launched into the integrity of the IPCC report by different bodies around the globe. The general conclusion was that the report was scientifically sound, but sloppy. "By and large, the IPCC has delivered a formidable summary of the current state of knowledge," said Maarten Hajer, the director of the Netherlands Environmental Assessment Agency. The important point was that the high-level messages were accurate, even if the many small errors were inexcusable. The IPCC had claimed that 55 per cent of the Netherlands lay below sea level when the real figure was 26 per cent. The report had stated that all Himalayan glaciers might melt by 2035, but this was an exaggeration. As for the number of Africans exposed to water shortage, the IPCC reported the figure as being 75–250 million people, whereas the investigations revealed that the answer was closer to 90–220 million.

Minor errors of this kind were not unheard of in science. As in most professions, points were lost for slip-ups and overreaching. But one of the reasons they received so much attention in the climate arena was because of the pressure placed on science by pseudo-politicians like Pachauri. Pachauri had built up expectations of a scientific world promising perfection and certainty. When it wobbled momentarily, it tarnished Pachauri's reputation and that of the group he represented. Their larger conclusions were still accurate. Scientific opinion may not have changed, but a valuable commodity had nevertheless been corroded: popular trust.

This point was made brutally clear by Geoffrey Boulton, a professor emeritus of geology at the University of Edinburgh. Boulton had been appointed by the British government to a panel of experts conducting a thorough review of the IPCC's findings. The panel cleared Professor Jones and his colleagues of misconduct, but Boulton's assessment of them was scathing. Certain scientists had overstepped their mark, he said. They had proceeded as if by "papal announcements: this is this and that is that and you have to accept it" without opening themselves up to full transparency.

The world was locked in impossible disagreement over climate change because the issue had been framed in the wrong way. The trouble was not with the science. The majority of professional scientists were of one mind on the probable drivers of climate change. But in pressing this point, some had claimed "certainty" for their findings when all they had was "beyond reasonable doubt". The latter by itself gave firm grounds for action.

4.

Framing climate change as a contest between two kinds of certainty – belief and scepticism – was dramatically satisfying but intellectually loose. It was dramatically satisfying because it made science glamorous – a battle of talking heads, Believers against Sceptics. It was intellectually loose because it took science out of its natural habitat and adapted it to the world of the Hollywood screenplay. The real strength of the scientific method lay in something which non-scientists had no reason to observe directly or participate in. It came from the small nudges among professors and the incremental improvements in understanding from experiments conducted year after year. It came from the fact that one lab had published in *Geosciences* but another had published an even better paper in *Nature*. When scientists from the two labs met at a conference in Cambridge, they contrived a third path which was even more fruitful and authoritative.

Climate science was absent from our lives because we lacked the technical expertise to understand its true dimensions. And yet we were spurred to judgement on scientific questions by the thrill of the mainstream media. We were drawn into debates between talking heads, zooming in on the media and missing the scientists. For both sides, what made someone an authoritative media personality was not the same as what made them an authoritative scientist. The best performers were those with sharp elbows who could muscle in on Hollywood.

They could fight in newsprint and on radio, on television and online. We were persuaded by their abilities under bright lights. Whether they were any good at science was a different matter entirely.

It is understandable why this new world emerged. There *were* climate insurgents, implacable sceptics who were unwilling to compromise their position on climate change no matter what. John Holdren, Obama's science adviser, had called them "heretics". It seemed necessary to target these fanatics and shoot them down intellectually much as Bush had done militarily with terrorists in his war on terror. But framing the problem in this way committed the same mistake Bush had. It focused on the people and missed the underlying process.

If we reframed the problem, we had a chance of resolving it. Our task was not to adjudicate on scientific *experiments* – this was the wrong system in focus. It was to judge the scientific *authority* of the person we were listening to. This was a longstanding and difficult question, but one that was actually worth asking. The meaning of carbon emissions – resolved in the minutiae of scientific experiment and statistical analysis – was the preserve of professional scientists. But this only underlined the fundamental political challenge: we had to respect both science *and* democracy. Once the scientific findings were clearly in view, the question arose of how to respond to them. What was the right balance between delegating power to scientists who understood the meaning of carbon emissions and giving the wider public the freedom to form their own judgement on how best to deal with climate change? It seemed undemocratic to delegate unfettered power to scientists to decide the fate of the economy and the environment. Yet it was hard to see how people could exercise impartial judgement when they were fixated on the media spectacle. This challenge was precisely what the climate debate *should* have been about, but it was wholly missing from public discussion.

In his sprawling history of democracy, John Keane shows that it has evolved through many forms to deal with questions of relative authority. In ancient Greece, democracies were direct. Scouts were sent around cities to tally up individual votes for every decision of civic importance. Voters in modern representative democracies, by contrast, elect parliamentary representatives to act on their behalf. Keane's concern was that democracy was evolving into a new beast: monitory democracy. Monitory democracy was government by excessive delegation: expert and special-interest groups taking over the job of ordinary voters.

It is important not to overstate the case, but one manifestation of this was the way scientists were being asked to give their opinion on non-scientific matters. In 2005, Tony Blair, then British prime minister, held a scientific conference on climate change in the lead-up to the G8 conference in Gleneagles. The conference was titled "Avoiding Dangerous Climate Change" and Blair handed the microphone to scientists to "identify what level of greenhouse gases in the atmosphere is self-evidently too much". This raised an interesting question about what constituted danger. Was it a scientific measure or a social one? Should a person be free to live in a more dangerous world if they freely chose? For sceptic Nigel Lawson the answer was yes – he preferred to adapt to danger. "I think the ordinary bloke has an instinctive sense that it wouldn't be too bad if the weather warmed up," he told a reporter. Even though Lawson spoke from the perspective of a man living in soggy England, his meaning was plain enough. Sceptics were often voicing something softer than radical disbelief in science. They were claiming that their democratic freedom to choose a dangerous future was being infringed.

Letting scientists set policy was one risk, but monitory democracy might also be brought about if we gave too much power to industries and their lobby groups. In their book *Merchants of Doubt*, Naomi Oreskes and Erik Conway argued that the political process on climate change was being distorted by concentrations of corporate power. The fossil-fuel industry was shaping public policy behind closed doors. These companies had no particular authority to decide voters' future, yet Oreskes and Conway found that they exerted a disproportionate influence.

These two arguments, from different sides of the political spectrum, essentially made the same point. Certain groups of people wielded large influence in areas where they had limited authority. So the real question was this: how to build democratic institutions which found a balance between delegating to scientists and respecting the freedom of voters to choose their own future?

In 2010, some of the most intelligent voices inside the British Conservative Party argued that they accepted the science but believed we needed to *adapt* to climate change. Taking pre-emptive action by phasing out fossil-fuel use was too expensive, they argued. "Even if we were to spend gazillions on alternative energy, covering our hills with windfarms, carpeting our plains with solar panels, damming every estuary with turbines, it would buy us only a few more decades," said Daniel Hannan. The argument was novel and illustrated why climate change was such a political shapeshifter. Even if we eventually agreed that a healthy democracy was one which respected science and knew how to use it properly, a new dilemma quickly surfaced. We then had to decide on the best technical and most cost-effective way forward.

CHAPTER 6

THE ALL-YOU-CAN-EAT GUIDE
to carbon slimming

There is a parable told about how the world ends. It begins with a man who lives in Texas. When he is young and fit, he lives off the land. As he grows older and richer, he becomes greedier and lazier. The Texan has lots of children and buys each of them a large car. One day a priest visits the Texan and tells him his lifestyle will destroy the Earth. His cars puff out smoke and each ton of smoke damages the planet. The more children he has, the more cars he buys, and the quicker he will destroy everything around him.

When the priest presents this dilemma to the Texan, he protests. "Why should I stop driving my car if my neighbour commits a far worse crime?" he asks. "He switches on his air conditioning so he can enjoy his log fire in summer!"

"Fair point," says the priest. He goes next door and asks the neighbour to turn off his air conditioning.

"Why should I turn off my air conditioning if it is my only pleasure in life? Go tell the lady across the road to stop flying to Bangkok twice a year." And so the argument continues until the priest realises he is on a hopeless quest. The world is filled with Texans, he reflects, and that is how the world ends.

In his pessimistic account of humanity's future entitled *Requiem for a Species*, the environmentalist Clive Hamilton tells a version of this parable. The purpose of the parable is to explain why the world is imperilled by climate change. It is too late to avert catastrophe, Hamilton tells us. The only thing left is to ponder where it all went terribly wrong. In the book Hamilton tells his readers the answer: we are being destroyed by our own wastefulness and greed.

> The situation we face has arisen not from the old working-class vice of excessive copulation but the modern middle-class vice of excessive consumption. And just as in later editions of his essay Malthus recognised that the natural checks of famine and war could be avoided by "moral restraint" in the form of postponement of marriage and abstinence, so the answer to the climate crisis lies in dis-interring the middle-class virtues of moderation and frugality.

It is noteworthy that Hamilton stands on Thomas Malthus's shoulders to build his case. Environmentalists have long relied on this eighteenth-century British economist to argue that economic growth will destroy the planet. What they never tell you, though, is that Malthus turned out to be spectacularly wrong.

1.

In 1798, a London publisher printed a book which would become one of the most famous treatises of its time. Its title was *An Essay on the Principle of Population, as It Affects the*

Future Improvement of Society, with Remarks on the Specula-tions of Mr Godwin, M. Condorcet, and Other Writers. Thomas Malthus had written the book as a warning that Britain was on the verge of economic and ecological collapse. The districts of St Giles, Whitechapel and Clerkenwell in the city of London were already overflowing with beggars and prostitutes, and the streets buckled with the weight of a burgeoning population. Excess had become so omnipresent that the word "slum" had been invented to capture the state of Britain's festering poorhouses. Unless population growth was radically curtailed, the country would be ruined. Violence would erupt. Food would be stockpiled and corpses would line the streets, increasing the risk of plague and disease. You had only to look around to see the way things were going.

The cause of Malthus's angst was the finite carrying capacity of the land. People bred more children than the land could cater for. Unless the population boom was stopped, Britain would very quickly run out of food. Malthus calcu-lated that Britain could not sustain more than 9 million peo-ple in 1800. "Bachelors and spinsters I decidedly venerate," declared Mr Fax, a literary embodiment of Malthus in Thomas Love Peacock's novel *Melincourt*. "The world is overstocked with featherless bipeds. More men than corn is a fearful pre-eminence, the sole and fruitful cause of penury, disease and war, plague, pestilence and famine."

Malthus's ecological predictions seemed reasonable enough, which is why it was so strange that they never came to pass. In fact, not only did England avoid Malthusian famine, but society moved quickly in the opposite direction: greater prosperity and a bigger population. By the mid-nineteenth century Britain had doubled its numbers and by 1901 the population was 30 million. These were not 30 million starving people, but 30 million people healthier and richer than at any other period in history. The real income of the average Englishman was 50 per cent higher in 1850 than 1750 (despite a trebling of the population), and, more significantly, the quality of life was vastly improved. The average calorie intake in Britain was a good measure of this. It finally rose in the nineteenth century from a level similar to that of primitive hunter-gatherer societies. In a nation of finite agricultural resources, how was this feat possible?

The paradox could be explained if you took into account an invisible phenomenon transforming the British economy: the Industrial Revolution. Malthus's lifespan from 1766 to 1834 almost perfectly bookended Britain's coming of industrial age. There were many inventions during this time which radically changed the economy, but their significance was not fully apparent at the time. Take Watt's steam engine of 1776: it enormously increased the amount of work that could be accomplished by a single day's labour, but at the time its various uses were little understood. Then there was the rolling mill, and Henry Cort's version of it in particular, patented in 1783: it enabled the mass manufacture of iron sheets, which in turn had incredibly useful applications in everything from construction to household appliances. The cotton industry was also radically remade by the Industrial Revolution. In 1766 a pound of cloth took eighteen man-hours to produce. By 1866 the same amount of cloth could be produced in one and a half hours. The British population had grown, but British innovation had grown even faster.

The Industrial Revolution not only changed the productivity of a single worker, it also created benefits for the economy as a whole. The early telecommunications industry, for example, amplified the impact a single person could have over a sparse geography. France built its first signal telegraph line from Paris and Lille in 1794 and Morse gave them the language to communicate in 1832. The geographical challenge was also tackled by the invention in 1804 of the locomotive, which transformed the speed at which goods and people could be freighted across land. Who would have thought, wrote Thomas Babington Macaulay in the *Edinburgh Review* in 1830, "that stage-coaches would run from London to York in twenty-four hours, that men would be in the habit of sailing without wind, and would be beginning to ride without horses"?

The answer was that no one could have seen the Industrial Revolution coming. It was much easier to spot examples of greed and waste than it was to see the invisible relationships of economic productivity. If we were to look out from the drawing rooms of our gracious property on London's Fleet Street in 1798, there is every chance we would have seen things as Malthus did. His essay, after all, was merely expressing the majority view of Britain's educated upper-middle class. Malthus had no intention of being subversive or gloomy. "A more simple-minded, virtuous man ... than

Mr Malthus could not be found in all England," opined the society lady Harriet Martineau in her defence of Malthus against his Tory critics in the *Quarterly Review*. Malthus had not even been the first to spot the profuse waste and excessive consumption taking place outside his window. Forty years earlier another scholar, Robert Wallace, had published similar views in his *Various Prospects of Mankind, Nature, and Providence*.

There is something more delicious about the story of Thomas Malthus than the simple point that he missed the invisible processes of technological innovation. The Malthusian mistake was a perfectly human one. There is something about the waste and over-consumption story which is emotionally compelling. Perhaps this is because waste is easier to see; but human psychology is also part of it.

A clue to why Malthus was so convincing can be found in an essay written by a little-known Hungarian philosopher, Aurel Kolnai. Kolnai's 1927 essay "On Disgust" examined why humans were so drawn to the topic of excess, decay and decline. We were fascinated by stories of excess and wastefulness, he argued. We sought them out, even though we knew we would be shocked by the sheer extravagance. Kolnai argued that the fixation fed a psychological need. Excess was a metaphor for death and decay. Artists were intrigued by urban decay because it connoted the death of society. Tabloid newspapers recorded extravagance because it fed our fascination with life gone to seed. The symbols of excess attracted us as much as they repelled us. We were fixated on the subject, but it also clouded our thinking.

The error of the Malthusian magnifying glass might be brushed aside as little more than an honest sense of caution. After publishing his essay, for example, Malthus spent much of his career advocating for abstinence among the unmarried. This wasn't especially controversial at the time, although it did earn "Parson Malthus" some ridicule. Cobbett, a popular cartoonist, satirised the Malthusian perspective in the June 1831 edition of the *Twopenny Trash*. His strip, titled "Surplus Population", showed a gang of village elders drawing up the village mating plan with one of the conspirators, the Malthusian Sir Gripe Grindum, being pushed into the horse pond for his views.

But in certain circumstances the Malthusian magnifying glass led to dangerous and illiberal conclusions. The more sinister aspect of Malthus's ideas was the deprivation of welfare to the poor. The Tory prime minister William Pitt had proposed reforms to the Poor Laws in the 1790s which sought to further ease the pressure on society's destitute. By extending the basic wage to poor men and widows with multiple children, Pitt had hoped to improve their chance of survival. Malthus argued these laws subsidised the population crisis. A basic wage artificially inflated the livelihood of the poor, who would otherwise be wiped out by war and pestilence. "Nature's table is full, and that, in consequence, the new-born child of a pauper should be starved," wrote the Malthusian William Maginn in *Fraser's* in 1830. It was a harsh view and one that would inform Charles Darwin's theory of the survival of the fittest a few decades later. Malthus's theory provided a justification for why the surging poor should be culled.

2.

Malthus's assertion that a growing population led to environmental catastrophe would have been correct under one scenario: technological stasis. If nothing had changed in the productivity of labour, then over-breeding would naturally tend to famine. It was a case of simple arithmetic. "Population, when unchecked, increases in a geometric ratio," Malthus observed in the first edition of his essay. "Subsistence increases only in an arithmetic ratio." The problem was that technological stasis was an incorrect starting point. Malthus had overlooked the dynamic innovation bubbling through the British economy. People had not become less greedy over the nineteenth century; they had just become more efficient.

If Malthus had made his observation in any previous century, he would have been right. Technological innovations had always developed, but they were often abandoned at moments of greatest natural stress, thereby winding back progress.

Take the case of England in the Middle Ages. If you had to be transported to the Middle Ages, the year you would choose to visit would be 1200. Village life buzzed with the sound of travelling merchants, fairs and markets. Things had a way of balancing out under the guidance of the feudal lord and lady. You offered your labour to cultivate their land. In exchange they fed you. Everyone played their part. A good feudal lord and lady made sure their serfs received enough food and had a job to do. The farmer grew the wheat, which was turned into flour by the miller. The baker made the bread, which would feed everyone in the village. If there was abundance one year, the surplus would be traded with the neighbouring village. Windmills, watermills, bridges and footpaths dotted the landscape, and in the background monasteries sounded with the hum of learning.

Had you chosen to arrive a generation later, you would have found an even bigger village. It was bigger because the miller, the baker and the brewer had all thought the same thing: an idyllic life was not worth much without someone to share it with. Prosperity led to fecundity. New mouths arrived and more mouths meant more demand for the farmer to reap and the baker to bake. It also put more pressure on the land to produce.

The feudal lord may have been able to accommodate this for a while. But as cultivation extended to the edges of his estate, and the less productive land, the amount of grain which could be harvested from a single acre diminished. The lord not only faced economic pressures to produce, he also faced legal pressure from his sovereign. In 1267, the Statute of Marlbridge was passed, introducing the term "waste" for the first time into English, to describe land or goods which were not being used to full potential. Waste, by malice or negligence, had become an actionable offence.

The problem was that as things became difficult, people became more protective rather than more productive. This response was hard for the Statute of Marlbridge to outlaw. Had you timed your visit for the early 1300s, you would have found a precarious existence. Not only was there less cooperation, but things were made worse by natural disasters. In 1315, and again in 1317, bad weather left wheat crops rotting on their stems. Villagers were forced to feed off the unripened seeds of dead crops. Mothers abandoned unwanted children, and the elderly were left to fend for themselves. Within a few decades, famine turned to disease. The Black Death swept through the country in the 1340s, and plague returned in the 1360s after another bout of bad weather. By the end of the century, the population of England had been whittled away to the same number as in 1200.

Matt Ridley points out in his book *The Rational Optimist* that the correct response to prosperity and growth should have been greater specialisation. As the baker's family grew, a market for nannies should have arisen to give the baker's wife more time to help in the bakery. There was also a commercial opportunity to sell baby food in the village. If the families of bakers, millers and farmers did not need to spend an hour each evening crushing carrots into baby mush, then they would be able to work an extra hour in the field. They would also have the time to pursue the creative ideas they had imagined but had put off because they were too busy.

Medieval England was so economically and socially rigid compared to what would come later that none of these new possibilities fully developed. There was limited innovation in work practices, and fancy tools were quickly discarded. Instead of experimenting with new ways of doing things, in periods of acute stress the villagers reverted to the instincts which had gripped them in the past: they became more self-sufficient rather than better at specialisation. By working harder, they actually became less creative and less productive. They tried to keep everything in-house when they should each have focused on what they were good at and delegated the rest. It was specialisation and delegation that led to technological innovation and increased expertise. Self-sufficiency made the village highly vulnerable to catastrophe. And in a rigid social world where people didn't follow through on their creative ideas, Malthusian predictions often turned out to be correct.

Yet by the eighteenth century, the tyranny of feudal economics was being dismantled. Robert Heilbroner gives a lively account of just how novel the social changes were in his classic economic history of the world, *The Worldly Philosophers*. Heilbroner's examples stretch from the Middle Ages to the start of the Industrial Revolution. Under the medieval guild system, for example, new inventions had been stifled. "The idea that one master guildsman might produce a better product than his colleagues was regarded as treasonable," Heilbroner wrote. In one case in the sixteenth century, a "wonder workshop" had been privately established containing over 200 looms which weaved day and night. It was the world's first mass-manufacture textile facility, which was even equipped with a kitchen to service its hungry weavers. When the textile guilds found out, they protested about its extraordinary efficiency. As a result it was outlawed.

In another case, Heilbroner wrote, the Privy Council had denied a revolutionary patent for the stocking frame and ordered the device be abolished. It had promised to rapidly increase the productivity of wool-spinners. The Privy Council's complaint was that the invention was so good it threatened to put thousands of them out of work.

Inventions such as these did not cluster in the late sixteenth century by fluke. They were brought into being by changes in the organisation of society. Land, which had once been enjoyed commonly, was being turned into private property for the first time. It could be sold in allotments to the bidder who offered the highest price. Privatising land was a radical social change. Aristocratic families had been custodians of land for centuries, but privatisation turned land into an object of commerce. This enabled technological development in the agricultural sector and especially wool production, which was very profitable. At first the privatisation of feudal land was deeply unpopular because it created a generation of landless, wandering serfs. "Where [forty] persons had their livings, now one man and his shepherd hath all," complained one John Hales in 1549.

But the wandering serfs were a temporary phenomenon. Just as land had become a saleable commodity by the sixteenth century, so too had labour. Serfs, no longer farmers and not yet factory workers, wandered the country selling their labour to budding entrepreneurs. This was so novel that the English parliament did not know how to respond. At first it introduced workhouses to localise the problem of unemployment. Paupers were forced to stay in their home town, and if they wandered off for work, they would be whipped or mutilated. The system was soon abandoned as the demand for labour grew, filling the country with new types of industry.

The third commodity which emerged during this time was financial capital. Capital had always existed, but it had not been easily accessible. As the market economy emerged, commercial lending flourished and businessmen took out loans to convert their ideas into industry.

These three components – land, labour and capital – became the foundations for a new way of living centred on a dynamic market economy rather than a feudal hierarchy. The market economy was hard to see because it emerged gradually, piece by piece, but once it was in place there was no going back. Technologies that had previously been stymied by feudal hierarchy were given oxygen for the first time.

One author who recorded these changes was the Scottish economist Adam Smith. In the opening of his 1776 classic, *An Inquiry into the Nature and Causes of the Wealth of Nations*, Smith was acutely aware that he was documenting a new phenomenon. "Five years have seldom passed away," he wrote, "in which some book or pamphlet has not been published pretending to demonstrate that the wealth of the nation was fast declining; that the country was depopulated, agriculture neglected, manufactures decaying and trade undone."

But the world had changed, Smith argued. Rather than following the orders of feudal lords, the economy was now being organised by the invisible hand of a modern market economy. It was governed by two interconnected principles. The first, as we have just seen, was mobility of labour. Smith observed that workers moved to those corners of the market where there was greatest need. If there was a shortage of watches one year, workers rushed to the watches sector. If another year people wanted spinach, workers packed up their stalls and started selling spinach.

The second connected principle was competition. When people wanted spinach, many people rushed to offer their services. If society had a single spinach vendor, then that vendor alone would have the power to control the price. But in a world of many vendors, the price was always kept in check. The beauty of competition was that it encouraged invention and adaptation. Vendors were constantly seeking ways to bring down the price of spinach. Often their answer came in the form of innovation. Maybe they discovered new machines to harvest spinach more quickly or methods of organising the workforce which improved production. Either way, the freedom to invent these new ways of doing things distinguished this period from previous epochs of history. Malthus had been right in his description of a pre-industrial world, but with the creative forces of invention now unleashed, things had changed for good.

Trade had always existed, but a market economy which respected private property was new. It allowed waste and excess to become perversely valuable. Population gluts could be turned into a fluid, mobile labour force. Unused wastelands could be turned into harvestable properties.

And traditional practices which had stubbornly persisted for centuries could be overturned by innovative new ideas. By the late seventeenth century, the same Privy Council which had rejected the patent for the stocking frame decided that it had become so valuable that it prohibited its export.

3.

There was a simple test for checking whether Adam Smith was correct and Malthus wrong. You could wait for the next time finite resources became a problem and study whether the invisible hand was able to bring about change. If it did, the market economy might be more reliable than Malthusians predicted. If it failed, the debate was over.

One of the next chances came in the late nineteenth century, as the Industrial Revolution reached its zenith. Coal had fed the world's industrial progress up to this point, but in 1865 a young economist called William Stanley Jevons published a bestseller called *The Coal Question* in which he questioned whether this was sustainable. The coal problem, Jevons argued, was much worse than Malthus's food problem. "A farm, however far pushed, will under proper cultivation continue to yield forever a constant crop," argued Jevons. "But in a mine ... the produce once pushed to the utmost will soon begin to fail and sink towards zero." Britain, in other words, was running out of coal.

Jevons understood the problem of Britain's coal shortage at first hand. As a 21-year-old, he had abandoned his studies in natural sciences in London and travelled to Sydney. The young Jevons took employment there as a mining assayer. His job was to inspect ore and mineral deposits along the country's east coast and assess their value. The job interested him for a while, but then he found himself wondering about the state of his own country's natural resources. In *The Coal Question,* he laid out his analysis of Britain's economic prospects given its reserves.

Jevons looked to the future by considering the archaeology of past production. He took a measure of how quickly the demand for coal had grown over the previous decades. He then examined the depth of Britain's reserves. The calculations quickly revealed that these supplies would eventually run out. Since the economy was heavily dependent on coal for progress, "peak coal" would destroy the British Empire. It is "useless to think of substituting any other kind of fuel for coal," he added. "It is thence simply inferred that we cannot long continue our present rate of progress." Britons "must either leave the country in a vast body, or remain here to create painful pressure and poverty".

The Coal Question made Jevons an instant international celebrity. His prime minister, William Gladstone, ordered a Royal Commission to investigate the problem. On both sides of the Atlantic, newspapers ran with the story of peak coal. "The sensational topic of the day," announced the *New York Times* in 1866, "is unquestionably about the scant supply and exorbitant prices of coal."

Jevons's prediction set the British and American public alight. As news spread, people queued for miles to grab their last supplies. A black market emerged and scalpers sold coal for exorbitant prices so the rich could warm their houses for the last time. In Pennsylvania, the president of the Erie Railway Company put out a circular to customers. The company would be selling what limited supply of bitumous coal they had in their mines. Interested customers were advised to wait near the tracks at Port Jervis.

What Jevons had discovered about Britain was correct. The country's coal reserves had peaked and were in decline. What he had missed, though, was why this wasn't such a problem. While the world had run out of coal in one corner, entrepreneurs in another had found a more than adequate substitute. Several years before the publication of *The Coal Question,* salt farmers in Pennsylvania and West Virginia had discovered a strange thing as they drilled for brine water, which they evaporated for salt. Occasionally their drills would uncover a black liquid or a gas which was often packaged as waste or sold as lighter fluid. America's salt farmers didn't have much use for the stuff, but a young entrepreneur, John D. Rockefeller, thought it had much greater value.

In 1868, Rockefeller struck a deal with the Lake Shore Railroad in New York that allowed him to take advantage of the new discoveries. In exchange for a guaranteed volume, the Lake Shore Railroad offered Rockefeller a discount on his freight costs. Rockefeller then did a similar deal with other railroad companies across the country. With these contracts in place and access to a few of these sites, Rockefeller incorporated the Standard Oil Company of America.

Rockefeller's innovation was to turn a natural phenomenon into a marketable product. Until that point, most com-
bustible fuels had been things you could dig up and put on
the back of a truck. The idea that a liquid which spouted out
of the ground in unpredictable locations could be packaged
into a commodity and sold was new. A barrel of oil became
a technological substitute for a ton of coal. It may not have
been obvious to Jevons at the time, but he had made a similar mistake to the one Malthus made half a century earlier.
He had assumed technological stasis by looking too hard
into the past. By focusing too heavily on one thing, he had
missed the entrepreneurial processes shaping the future.

4.

Fears about the Industrial Revolution faded as the world
descended into two world wars. But the world did not get
very far into the post-war recovery before the magnifying
glass of Malthusian pessimism returned. As Europe
repaired itself and the populations of India and China
ascended out of poverty, the belief that the planet would
run out of resources once again took hold.

To all appearances, this was the lesson of the 1950s and
'60s. Americans were consuming more heavily than ever
before and the aspirational middle classes of Europe and
Australia were buoyed by the prospects of mimicking the
modern American consumer. If the world's most populous
nations, China and India, joined the party, then the planet
was surely doomed. Ergo, Malthus had proved his point.

In 1968, the ecologist Garrett Hardin wrote a seminal essay called "The Tragedy of the Commons", which was first delivered as a lecture to the American Association for the Advancement of Science at Utah State University. Its message was the same as that of the bestselling book that year, *The Population Bomb* by Paul Ehrlich. Ehrlich and Hardin were both self-confessed Malthusians. Their message gripped the popular imagination because it described what everyone thought each time they walked into a mall and saw a person weighed down with a ridiculous number of shopping bags. The world was growing too quickly and if we were going to maintain a healthy planet something had to give. Ehrlich and Hardin argued that the place to begin was by stopping population growth.

"The population problem," Hardin declared in his essay, "cannot be solved in a technical way, any more than can the problem of winning the game of tick-tack-toe." Hardin's point was that technology offered no solution to the ecological crisis of the 1960s. People seemed to have an irresistible desire to bear children which only weighed the planet down further. Every time a woman gave birth to a child, the ecological footprint of that family spiralled upwards. In fact, if you assumed that the child in turn would possess an irresistible urge to procreate, then the ecological cost of bearing children was exponential.

Hardin made his point by asking his reader a very simple question: "Has any cultural group solved this practical problem at the present time, even on an intuitive level? One simple fact proves that none has: there is no prosperous population in the world today that has, and has had for some time, a growth rate of zero."

By some curious twist of fate, 1968 was the last year when Hardin could have made this statement and been right. After 1968, the population boat not only halted, it began to turn around. First it was obscure nations like the Cook Islands and the Northern Mariana Islands that experienced zero population growth rates. Then more formidable names joined the party: Bulgaria, Ukraine, Germany, Japan. These were nations which were not only growing more slowly; in some cases their populations were actually in decline. Within a few decades, the problem some countries faced was actually the opposite of population growth. With an aging population, how would the scarce younger generation support the aged?

Ehrlich and Hardin had missed the aging population phenomenon because changes in the underlying demographics of a population were extremely hard to see. As early as the Great Depression, Warren Thompson, an American sociologist at Miami University, had noticed that there were differences in the demographics of countries. Thompson split the world into three groupings. Group A countries (the United States and Western Europe) seemed to have a gradually declining population. Group C countries (most of Asia, Latin America and Africa), which made up three-quarters of the world, seemed to be exploding in size. Group B (Eastern Europe) sat somewhere in between. Thompson had no way of explaining why different populations behaved differently. From a Malthusian perspective, though, the difference was irrelevant. Since the vast majority of the world sat in Group C, what was happening in Western Europe did not affect the future of the planet.

The conclusion that there was no relationship between the populations of Group A, B and C countries was generally accepted by demographers. In 1934, a French demographer, Landry, published *La Revolution demographique* in which he made this case. The difference between the groups, he argued, could probably be explained by entrenched cultural differences in the population base. As the 1950s turned into the 1960s, however, a surprising phenomenon emerged. Countries from the Group C demographic began to migrate to Group B, and Group B countries were migrating to Group A. The world's population seemed to be changing under the influence of an invisible process. The process acquired a special name, demographic transition theory.

The new theory explained why the world's population would not continue to grow indefinitely. Instead, it seemed that as countries became more wealthy, their population size steadied, then began to shrink. To see this clearly you needed statistical data, not tours to shopping malls. Several factors contributed to stabilising populations. One notable factor was improvements in infant mortality. New life-saving technologies gave mothers greater certainty that their children would not die young. This reduced the impulse to have more children. A second factor was improvements in female education and inclusion in the workplace. As women became wealthier and more liberated, their desire to have a school-yard full of children shrunk.

The invisible processes at work in demographic transition theory were denied by Ehrlich and Hardin. In one scathing remark, Ehrlich wrote that "the most serious of [*Nature* editor] Maddox's many demographic errors is his invocation of a 'demographic transition' as the cure for population growth in Asia, Africa, and Latin America". Within a few decades the data suggested differently.

Hardin and Ehrlich had their hearts in the right place. The problem was that viewing the world through a fixed magnifying glass led to some very dangerous outcomes. Through the 1960s and '70s the urgency with which some people were gripped by the ecological challenge of the population bomb led to some rash conclusions. It is not possible to "avoid the evils of population without relinquishing any of the privileges [we] now enjoy", Hardin told his readers in "The Tragedy of the Commons". He was particularly against the idea that people should have a right to family life. The right had been enshrined in the Universal Declaration of Human Rights of 1948 but Hardin had found it "intolerable". If people continued to bear children, then legislation might be necessary to curb people's freedoms. "Laws requiring compulsory abortion," Ehrlich added, "could be sustained under the existing US Constitution if the population crisis became sufficiently severe to endanger the society."

Compulsory abortion was never introduced in the United States, but in countries like India, with weaker legal protections, human rights were more easily abused. In *The Rational Optimist*, Matt Ridley points out that Sanjay

Gandhi, acting under the leadership of his mother who was India's prime minister at the time, used financial incentives to lure 8 million poor Indians to take vasectomies. In some extreme cases, more stick than carrot was applied to sterilise the population. In one episode noted by Ridley, every male in the Indian village of Uttawar was rounded up by the police and sterilised. The community reacted by defending the neighbouring town of Pipli, at which point the police opened fire. When asked whether they regretted the incident, a government official later said that he was fighting a war on "people pollution".

"If some excesses appear, don't blame me," he told reporters. "Whether you like it or not, there will be a few dead people."

5.

But Malthus's legacy lived on! In the 1980s, Ehrlich returned to public attention with a repackaged version. This time the problem was resource scarcity. Ehrlich's latest peg for his theory was a report published by the global environmental think-tank the Club of Rome in 1972. *The Limits to Growth* painted a devastating picture of the end of the twentieth century. While Stanley Jevons had once predicted peak coal in Britain, now the world was running out of basic commodities. Oil, copper, zinc, tin and gold were all part of the list which Ehrlich boldly predicted were bound to run out.

The Club of Rome authors had come to their conclusions much as Stanley Jevons had more than a century before. They took the short-term historical record and projected it into a static future. This time they were aided by an enormous computer model known as World3. The prospects for future resource prices were, as you might expect in a stationary world, alarming.

In 1980, an economist called Julian Simon approached Ehrlich with an enticing proposition which directly challenged the findings of the Club of Rome. Simon offered Ehrlich a wager. Pick any five raw materials, and any time period greater than twelve months, and Simon bet that their prices would decline over that period. It was a $1000 bet. Two hundred dollars' worth of each of the five materials was purchased on paper. If prices rose after adjusting for inflation, Simon would pay Ehrlich the difference. If prices for the materials fell, Ehrlich owed Simon. Ehrlich agreed to the bet and picked tin, tungsten, nickel, chromium and copper. He set the time period for the wager at one decade.

When 1990 came around, it turned out that Ehrlich owed Simon rather than the other way around. (The sum was US$576.07.) Simon had won because he appreciated a flawed assumption in the *Limits to Growth* thesis. Simon had predicted that new exploration sites as well as new technologies to mine existing sites would offset the problem of resource scarcity. There was an element of luck in Simon's victory. There was a chance that some resources might just run out. In the nineteenth century, for example, England had been scarce of timber which it needed for ship masts. In that case, the solution had not been the discovery of new forests or better ways to fell timber, but substitute materials with which to build. Relating this to the Simon–Ehrlich wager, there was a chance that tungsten might run out, but that the world would find a way to fill the gap.

Ultimately, though, Simon's point was similar to the one that had guided Adam Smith and John D. Rockefeller. They had invested faith in the invisible processes of technological innovation. By contrast the Malthusian perspective seemed to open up a bottomless pit of woe. Anything, in theory, could become an object of Malthusian limitation. Point the magnifying glass at coal and you worried that it would soon run out. Point it at tin and the most important thing in the world was to tell people that we had to limit our use of it. The difficulty with Malthusianism was it often distracted us from the bigger picture – the one which included the dynamic and inventive processes constantly competing to replace these objects. The Stone Age didn't end because the world ran out of stones.

A more sophisticated version of this doomsaying was when a Malthusian pointed to a limit on *capacity*. A lake had a limit on its capacity to carry fish in the same way that the atmosphere had a limit on its capacity to carry carbon. When the Malthusian dilemma was framed in this way, the mistakes were the same but they took more effort to be revealed. Climate change is a classic instance of this.

In 2010, Tim Jackson of the University of Surrey published a book called *Prosperity without Growth,* in which the Malthusian case for climate action was neatly articulated. Climate change, Jackson argued, demonstrated the limit of economic growth. Since modern economic development was entirely dependent on carbon emissions and the atmosphere had a limited carrying capacity for carbon, the planet was doomed unless economic growth was stopped.

Jackson was not the first person to have connected climate change to economic growth. George Monbiot, a journalist with the *Guardian*, had argued that climate change was among the reasons why we needed "an ordered and structured downsizing of the global economy".

Jackson had come to his conclusion by dividing the carbon economy into its three chief drivers: population, each person's carbon consumption (that is, their affluence) and the level of technology which sat behind every ton emitted. The formula Jackson used for the carbon economy was as follows:

$I = P \times A \times T$, where

I is the carbon impact on the environment

P is the global population

A is the average level of income (affluence) per person

T is the technology factor, calculated as the carbon intensity of every dollar of economic activity.

This formula was common sense. If you wanted to limit the amount of carbon in the atmosphere, you had to know where carbon came from and reduce one (or all) of these three drivers. The most basic driver was the world's population. Jackson conceded the ethical problems with limiting the population that Hardin and Ehrlich had come up against forty years earlier. Because the world's population was hard to control, Jackson accepted that it would rise until the end of the century, after which point demographic transition theory predicted it would begin to stabilise. Since the world was currently filled with about 7 billion people and the United Nations predicted the global population would stabilise at around 9 billion, population was a powerful driver of carbon emissions but one that was hard to control.

The second driver of carbon emissions was how much the average citizen consumed – what might be called the affluence factor. When you divided the world's Gross Domestic Product (GDP) by the global population, Jackson found that the average citizen earned about US$5900 a year. This had grown historically at about 1.4 per cent per annum. If it continued to rise, the world's carbon emissions would continue to grow.

The third factor in Jackson's equation was the carbon intensity of each dollar earned. Jackson calculated this by taking the world's total emissions and dividing them by the world's GDP. The result was that the carbon efficiency of the global economy had only improved at about 0.7 per cent annually over the last two decades. This rate of improvement was supremely insufficient given the limits scientists had placed on the carrying capacity of the earth. And since technology had historically been so poor at reducing carbon emissions, the idea that it would save us now was "nothing short of delusional". Jackson concluded that what was needed was a new way of enjoying prosperity without any economic growth. "There is as yet no credible, socially just ecologically sustainable scenario of continually growing incomes for a world of 9 billion people," he wrote.

On the face of it, the Malthusian case for climate action was extremely strong. History showed that technology had failed to reduce the carbon intensity of energy. Yet in fact Jackson was viewing the carbon economy through a distorting lens. By boiling things down to the "average citizen", he had missed much of the complexity of the world's energy sector. The average citizen was an academic fiction. In practice the world was divided between rich and poor regions.

The best way to see this complexity was to examine the statistics of the International Energy Agency. The organisation kept detailed statistics on each country's carbon intensity going back several decades. What became evident the closer you looked was that the carbon trajectory of rich countries in Europe and North America tracked a very different path to the more impoverished regions of Africa, Latin America and Asia. Throughout the 1970s and '80s, the carbon intensity of virtually every developed economy – the measure of carbon emissions per dollar of GDP – declined as the invisible hand transformed the energy profile of these countries. In the developing world, however, the world's poorest billion people were using more energy as they ascended the ladder of economic opportunity.

The technological transition was largely spurred by the oil shocks of the 1970s. As oil became more expensive, economies switched to alternative fuels to power their growth. In the 1970s, the rich world drew a large proportion of its energy from coal and oil. By 2007, a chunk of this consumption had switched from oil to gas. This was significant since gas had a lower global warming potential than oil. It was true that the total level of carbon emissions in these countries had risen and that coal and oil were still large contributors. But the counterintuitive insight was that these economies were not as technologically static as Jackson had suggested. Their energy sectors were changing and, in a number of rich-world countries, the absolute emissions per person were declining.

To get a better sense of these technical transitions in action, you had to look at each economy in detail. Take France, for example. France had a long scientific association with nuclear energy and therefore avoided the anti-nuclear sentiment which flooded Europe in the 1970s. When the oil price spiked, French business and government made a concerted decision to change the base of their energy economy. They built nuclear power plants across the country and eventually fed electricity throughout the continent. Not only did this make France one of the world's largest electricity exporters, but the carbon intensity of its economy today is about half what it was in 1971, which means the French emit less carbon into the atmosphere each year than they did four decades ago.

The story was similar in Britain. In the 1980s, Britain went through a series of financial reforms that switched its energy base from coal to gas. Its carbon intensity and absolute carbon emissions headed in a similar direction to that of France, so that the average Briton produced about 20 per cent *less* carbon emissions per capita in 2007 than in 1971. Iceland was another case in point. It modernised in the 1990s from an economy fed by fish to a financial hub. New investment flowed into the country's geothermal and hydroelectric assets so that these technologies supplied close to three-quarters of the country's power. Similar stories could be told across Europe, the United States and elsewhere. Jackson's average citizen, though, had such poor statistics because the developing world had not yet reached its moment of technological transition.

The story of how a richer world could also be a cleaner one was known to many economists as the Environmental Kuznet's Curve. It applied to environmental economics what the economist Simon Kuznet had famously observed in development economics: economic inequality increased as a country became wealthier, but only up to a point. Thereafter, inequality tended to decrease. For the environment, the story was slightly more complicated because not all environmental commodities (such as water and land) followed this curve and improvements didn't happen automatically. But the point was that things were more nuanced than the Malthusian picture suggested. As people became wealthier, they consumed more energy, but they could afford to move to more efficient and cleaner sources.

6.

The point of all this was *not* that we needed to do nothing to address climate change. It was that we had to ask ourselves the right question. Was dealing with climate change really a choice between the environment and the economy? Or did that way of framing the problem present a false choice and distract us from the effort to accelerate technological change?

The Malthusian argued that climate change was all about material consumption. To solve the problem we needed to purge the excesses of modern consumerism. We had to cut back on the cakes we ate, the cars we drove, the flights we took and so on. Climate change represented the tyranny of unnecessary things in our lives. If we removed the things, then we removed the problem.

Walk out the door and you could *see* why we had an environmental catastrophe on our hands, they argued. There were too many people walking around the planet. Nor was it just the sheer numbers of people that made things so bad for the environment, it was what these people did with their time. People these days ate too much, flew too much, earned too much money and had too many children. Tally it all up and you were left with a giant cloud of carbon floating around the atmosphere. If you wanted to stop climate change, you had to tackle the root of the problem: procreation and human wastefulness.

An alternative view disputed that this was the correct system in focus. Cutting consumption and reducing our flights were excellent things to do for various social and moral reasons. Greed, you could argue, weakened communities, harmed our personal health and skewed our sense of self ... but adding climate change to the list was a red herring. The point could be demonstrated by a simple thought experiment. If we ate all day and needlessly flew around the world, we would be wasting time and resources. But if these activities were powered by a carbon-neutral source, they wouldn't make a whit of difference to the climate. It was carbon, not energy, which mattered. Excessive consumption was gluttonous, but this was a different issue from climate change.

This alternative point of view embraced the importance of innovative ideas and entrepreneurship. Technology did not arise by fluke. It was carefully cultivated through systems and processes that could easily disappear if they were not recognised and nurtured. The Middle Ages bore witness to that. Entrepreneurship was not something a nation could buy off the shelf. It was a way of thinking about the world – a shift in culture and temperament rather than a public-policy program. It came from a willingness to pursue creative ideas and evolve solutions to problems. It functioned by means of an invisible hand pulling ideas from the surplus over here and adding them to the deficit over there. It involved a more optimistic view of society's ability to adapt to problems, but it was not something to be taken for granted. Humans had always proven inventive. What had sometimes been lost was our conviction that this was the best way to approach the world.

It is possible that the transformation which will take place to tackle climate change will be the carbon equivalent of the demographic transition we witnessed half a century ago. It may happen more quickly than we expect. Eastern Europe made the demographic transition to a falling population in half the time it took Western Europe. So too might the developing world make the carbon transition to a low-carbon economy quicker than any time in history. Many things need to happen before we reach this, but the key point is that climate change is not as insoluble a problem as the Malthusians suggest. If seen through a morally tinted lens, as a problem of greed and waste, it is an exhausting prospect, but seen as a technological problem it is much more similar in character to the challenges humanity has successfully managed in the past.

7.

Now is a good moment to step back and consider how far we have travelled with the idea of reframing. I opened with a grand claim: by changing the way we see our trickiest problems, we have a better chance of solving them. *Reframe* began with events from the 1990s and early 2000s. Change the topic – from finance, to terrorism, to immigration – and the mistake was always the same: we sought comfort in shiny objects and we missed the deeper processes at play.

We tend to think that complex problems are solved by making things simpler. *Reframe* delivers the opposite conclusion: simplification can make hard problems harder. In a way, that's what connects the three dimensions of our climate analysis over the last few chapters. At each stage we have reframed the problem by trusting people with more, not less, complexity. Take the weather/climate reframe. The weather is simple to see, but the climate is the accurate system in focus. By zooming in on the weather, a Kumi Naidoo and a Christopher Booker find themselves on the same side. They swim with the tide of events, but they make no progress in changing understanding.

Then take the science/democracy reframe. We divide the world into two spheres of existence: Believers and Sceptics. Yet too few of us have the qualifications in climate science to speak from first principles. It is more honest to accept that we cannot speak authoritatively about expert science, but that we should manage carefully the proper delegation of authority. This is a more subtle approach than Believer versus Sceptic, but it is also more truthful.

And finally there is the over-consumption/technology reframe. It's simple to focus on modern wastefulness, but quite a different thing to consider the carbon intensity of consumption. The two appear similar but are actually quite different. In a world of carbon-neutral donuts, consumption is not a climate problem.

Reframing often means trusting that ordinary people are more intelligent than they are sometimes assumed to be. The lesson of the Duncker candle problem is that this trust is not unreasonable. People are drawn to instant gratification, but they are not necessarily irrational. Although we may get distracted by what's visually compelling and bright, we rarely make the same mistake twice.

In our final chapters I want to take that idea one step further. I will consider objects which are not visually compelling, but conceptually compelling. Even the visually impaired can get sucked into the magnifying glass trap. To see why, we need to venture into new territory – foxes, hedgehogs and the lure of the single big idea.

CHAPTER 7

THE VALLEY OF DEATH

and how to climb out of it

I got a sense of how bad the drought was one day in 2009. I found myself sitting across the table from Mark Goldman at a Starbucks somewhere in Palo Alto, California. Goldman was wearing shorts and a T-shirt and telling me about his latest start-up company. Armageddon Energy was a business designed to bring solar energy to people's homes. The problem he wanted to solve, Goldman explained, was that solar panels were too expensive for people to put on their roof. His solution was to break down the cost into individual solar pads customised for kitchen appliances. Goldman's theory was that his pads allowed people to enter the market in an affordable way via a solar-powered refrigerator or a solar-powered kettle. By diffusing the cost, he was going to crack the domestic solar-energy market in a big way and retire early in Florida.

I felt bad for Goldman. After he gave me his spiel, it was obvious he was struggling to raise cash. Venture capitalists thought the market was too small. Commercial banks thought the market was too risky. It seemed a good idea to me, but Goldman should have had a better sense of that than I did. He had been a special adviser to the US Environmental Protection Agency, worked in the White House, set up five companies in the last twenty years, and come near the top of his MBA class at Stanford University. His classmates had taken the safe option and were rolling in money at investment banks and Fortune 500 companies. Goldman had shunned millions to make billions, but had ended up sitting on the other side of a table from me. You could say the problem was that his idea was rotten, but he wasn't the only one struggling in Silicon Valley. He invited me to a networking event that evening to meet other entrepreneurs with the same problem. It was not the financial crisis which was killing the clean-tech sector, Goldman said as we got up to leave. It was the Valley of Death.

1.

I had first become acquainted with the term "Valley of Death" on a train between Paris and London more than eighteen months before. I was in the dining carriage talking to Professor Michael Grubb from the University of Cambridge. Professor Grubb and I had been invited to a meeting at the offices of the Organisation for Economic Co-operation and Development in Paris. The OECD was one of the world's top economic think-tanks and not normally the place you went to talk about environmental matters. On this occasion, though, some of its top economists were intrigued by news that capital markets were facing a particular financial hurdle.

In theory, according to Adam Smith, the productive ideas of an economy, like low-carbon technologies, should have attracted the attention of profit-seeking investors. In

The Wealth of Nations, Smith had painted capitalism on a grand canvas where all the elements worked in harmony. The economy hummed along by dint of the invisible hand, moving investment into goods and services which people needed. Whereas in the seventeenth century only Louis XIV of France could feast on exotic cuisines when he sat down to dinner each night, within a few centuries anyone in Paris could enjoy the same privilege by virtue of the invisible hand.

Market economics brought interesting food ideas to life, but in the clean-tech sector – the corner of the market dedicated to new ways of generating electricity – theory was not aligning with practice as smoothly as you would hope. Although entrepreneurs like Mark Goldman were coming up with technically brilliant inventions, investors with solid-green credentials seemed reluctant to invest. The OECD had convened a meeting of finance and environment ministers from around the globe to work out why this was the case, and Professor Grubb had been invited to offer his explanation.

The Valley of Death, Professor Grubb explained to me on the train, was not a place you could visit. It was something an entrepreneur experienced when they went out to raise money for their ideas. If you were to visualise it, it would be a street fair where entrepreneurs stood at stalls offering their wares, and investors (venture capitalists, mainly) wandered around with their hands in their pockets.

The Valley of Death was so hard to see that most people assumed it didn't exist. The trap here was different to the one encountered earlier. Our first impressions weren't shaped by what we found visually compelling. They were shaped by what we found *conceptually* compelling – the idea that a totally free market might solve the world's technological problems without so much as a nudge from government. There was certainly something attractive about the idea. It had clean lines and projected great certainty about how the world worked. But it also had a fundamentalist aspect to it, blind to some of the hidden humps and bumps which entrepreneurs could encounter on the path to success. Certainly, entrepreneurs in many sectors surmounted such hurdles without any help from government. But the case of the new energy sector was more complex.

The Valley of Death did not appear on Bloomberg data streaming across computer screens or on the floor of the New York Stock Exchange. Most venture-capital transactions were private deals, and not recorded publicly. To the extent that it existed at all, it was verified by the gossip of entrepreneurs and investors muttering over coffee about how the market was so bad. The popular press had long recorded speculative bubbles, instances when investors were excessively attracted to a particular type of asset. The opposite – what we might think of as speculative droughts – went largely unnoticed.

Professor Grubb's description of the Valley of Death intrigued me. When you ventured into the annals of finance, you could find instances when a speculative drought had gripped technology investors before. In the 1970s, for example, it had descended on the pharmaceutical industry.

Doctors struggled to convince companies to release a drug called Cysteamine, even though it was a technically proven lifesaver. Cysteamine cured a rare genetic disorder in children called cystinosis which caused them to die of renal failure. Because there were only a few thousand cases of the disease worldwide, the pharmaceutical industry refused to invest in the drug and those few thousand kids suffered as a result. The scandal barely made the news. A decade later, a similar thing almost happened for children suffering from hypopituitary dwarfism, when a drug called Protropin was commercially delayed despite being able to prevent them becoming dwarfs.

Now the same phenomenon that had afflicted the biomedical industry in the 1970s and '80s appeared to be gripping the clean-tech sector. Was it that these technologies had no social value and the market was simply being efficient? That was one answer, but an alternative one posed the problem with more subtlety. Investors *wanted* to invest in clean-energy technologies, and entrepreneurs were eager to offer equity. The barrier to the market operating freely wasn't lack of desire; it was something else.

2.

To investigate what the barrier to clean-tech investment was, you had to travel to the frontiers of technological innovation. Among the best places to start was the United Arab Emirates. The UAE owned some of the world's richest oil fields, but in 2006, sheikhs from Abu Dhabi (the largest emirate) had decided to reinvest their money in building the world's first carbon-neutral city. It was called the Masdar City and it was something more than a US$22 billion publicity stunt. It was intended as a profitable venture, buying up ownership stakes in promising technologies and deploying them on a large scale.

Masdar City got off to a good start, but two years in, its chief engineers hit a surprising wall. You would think that lighting a desert city with solar power would be an easy thing to do. It turned out to be incredibly difficult.

The difficulty was first encountered on the small square-mile patch reserved for the city near Abu Dhabi airport. Masdar engineers had invited solar-panel providers from forty-one leading international companies to pilot their inventions over several months. What they soon discovered was that none of the panels had anything like their advertised performance in desert conditions. Despite the intense sun exposure they received, the panels were badly affected by other physical factors. Sand frequently blew in from the dunes, thickly covering them. This meant that even with the fierce Persian Gulf rays, the solar panels had the same performance in the desert as they did in a foggy English winter. "Most panel manufacturers test their product in climate-controlled labs," the infrastructure manager, Dr Sameer Abu-Zaid, later complained when the results were released. In real life these "perfect" laboratory conditions were entirely misleading.

I had never visited Masdar City myself, but this story was told to me by Karin Larsen, one of consultants hired by

Masdar to find commercially attractive technologies. As we spoke in Larsen's office in downtown San Francisco, what became obvious was that the clean-tech economy operated by different rules to the high-tech economy. Whereas you could manufacture a drug or an IT product and sell it anywhere in the world, the size of the potential market for clean tech was substantially smaller. You couldn't sell a clean-energy technology into the global economy; you could only sell it to *those parts* of the global economy which had the right physical conditions.

"What performs best in Abu Dhabi may be the exact opposite of what performs best in Germany or Japan, where it's a cooler climate," Larsen explained. Turn to any clean-energy technology and the logic was the same. After Larsen foraged for wind technologies from around the world, she discovered that the conditions in Abu Dhabi weren't ideally suited to wind power. When the city turned to onsite geothermal energy, it discovered that underground reservoirs weren't hot enough to drive turbines. Even water-purification technologies were subject to geographical constraints. The exceptionally high salinity of water in the Middle East meant that particular water membranes and water-treatment plants simply did not work.

Clean tech, by this measure, defied one of the central principles of economic globalisation. In *The World Is Flat* the journalist Thomas L. Friedman had argued that globalisation was making the world more similar. The same products could be bought and sold everywhere. As Friedman teed off at a golf course in Bangalore, the IBM and Microsoft buildings in the distance signalled where he could buy a computer identical to the one he had bought in America. If he wanted a meal, he could walk into a McDonalds in downtown New Delhi and buy a hamburger that looked and tasted the same as the one he had eaten at LAX airport. The world was getting flatter, Friedman contended, because the world was churning out commodity products. We lived in a single marketplace and we all consumed the same things.

That was true of many markets, but clean-energy technologies were an exception. If clean energy *could* have competed on the world stage, its business prospects might have been better. Cancer drugs and iPods were examples of technology products that worked equally well no matter which market they were sold into. By contrast, a clean-energy technology was so tied to the vagaries of weather and local geography that its potential market size was necessarily smaller. This was one reason why the sector faced a unique structural barrier.

Larsen had observed this as a customer. When I spoke to investors in Silicon Valley, they had learnt the same lesson the hard way. One venture capitalist had lost out in the biofuels business by neglecting it. When the CEO of a biofuels start-up had originally pitched a business idea to him, it had seemed brilliant. The business wanted to turn sugarcane into butanol, the chemical used to make paint. The business held the intellectual property of an enzyme that could do the fermentation faster than anything else on the market.

The venture capitalist had made his investment just as the company entered China to commence production. A few weeks later he received a call from the CEO. Something had gone terribly wrong. The sugarcane growing in the fields around the factory had been intended as feedstock for the bio-butanol production process. Instead it sat on the stalks rotting. It turned out to be a different genetic variant from the type they had been testing in the lab. It was possible to ship the required sugarcane from another part of the country, but the transportation costs made it uneconomical.

The fact that the business could not carry out its brief in China was the small problem. The bigger headache was that it showed the overall business model was unviable. The investors had originally assumed that they could expand to build bio-butanol factories across Asia, Europe and South America. They now realised their business was limited to the few locations around the globe close to that particular variant of sugarcane. By the time the venture capitalist got off the phone, he was looking to liquidate his stock.

There were ways of getting around the "small market" problem. On the Oakland side of San Francisco, just a few miles from Larsen's office, a little company called Makani Power had invented a wind-powered machine that tried to circumvent the importance of geography. The solution was a kite with an eighteen-foot wingspan, which was permanently flown around 2000 feet above the ground. At this altitude, wind speeds around the globe were thought to be more consistent. Electricity was generated by large propeller-like rotors and then transmitted by AC current down long tethers. The machine had been invented by Corwin Hardham, a semi-pro windsurfer, and had a touch of Benjamin Franklin's genius to it, though it had yet to achieve commercial deployment. It was a slightly hairbrained idea, but there were other technologies that weren't tied to their geography.

As I took my conversation with Larsen and tested it against the experience of other venture capitalists in Silicon Valley, they all seemed to concur. Clean-tech investing was unlike anything they had done before. Part of why it struggled to attract capital came down to the fact that the market size was unexpectedly small. The challenge could be summed up in one of Larsen's comments: "What works in desert climates won't necessarily work in temperate forest climates."

3.

The small-market problem is what the business world might think of as a volume problem. There is only so much biobutanol that can be generated in one location. There is a physical cap on how much solar energy can be generated in Abu Dhabi. This is not the case with, say, toothbrushes. The sale of toothbrushes is not limited by physical geography. It is limited by the number of teeth there are to brush in a city every night. That number could grow over time, but with clean tech the market size was fixed by supply constraints. That was the first reason why there was a Valley of Death in clean-tech investment.

There was a second reason why the sector stumped investors. It had to do with how much customers were willing to pay for low-carbon energy. Whereas consumers could always be persuaded to upgrade to a premium toothbrush, there was less scope to do this when you were selling a homogenous product like electricity.

In 1969, the challenge of pricing new ideas was considered by the Columbia business school professor Joel Dean. Dean wrote an article titled "Pricing Pioneering Products" in which he argued that a new product could set its price for customers in one of two ways. The first way was to be a *price taker*. This meant the product was priced in relation to similar products in the market. A new brand of ice-cream, for example, had to be a price taker because it was not genuinely novel. It had to compete with other types of ice-cream and this set the benchmark for what customers would pay.

The second way to price a new idea – by being a *price maker* – was only possible if a product was genuinely innovative. Because customers were eager to try the product for the first time, it could be priced at the level that "the traffic can bear". The first laptop computer was a price maker, for example, as was the first iPhone. (Dean then took his own advice and founded the high-end New York grocery store Dean & DeLuca, which charges very high prices for fancy, premium products.)

Dean argued that all CEOs wanted to be price makers, and that this was especially important for CEOs in high-tech industries. The cost of research and development of high-tech ideas was much higher than launching a new brand of ice-cream. Assuring an investor that a product could be a price maker, therefore, was often important to getting financial support. In an ideal scenario, a CEO could skim the market by enticing wealthy customers to pay a premium for early versions of the product. This gave the company learning experience which it could then use to cut costs and introduce a cheaper version of the product to mainstream customers.

In the healthcare and digital communication sectors, where venture capitalists had a lot of experience, premium pricing was common. New drugs and medical devices paid for themselves by first selling to customers who could afford to pay for special treatment. Likewise, early users of the iPhone often paid more for their devices than later customers did for the same device. In the energy sector, the challenge was more severe. From the first day a clean-energy product went on sale it was competing with a cheap direct substitute: fossil fuels.

When clean-energy technologies generated electricity, the product they were selling to customers was generic. Electricity was the same whether it came from burning coal or waiting for the wind to blow. And the cost of producing clean energy was much higher than for fossil-fuel energy.

In 2007, McKinsey, the global consulting company, had famously drawn the McKinsey Curve. It showed all the ways in which coal was cheaper than other energy technologies. Nuclear energy was uneconomical unless every ton of carbon emitted by a coal-fired power plant was about €10 more expensive. Solar, wind and biofuels became economical only if coal was about €20 more expensive per ton. And storing carbon under the ground through carbon capture and storage technologies was not commercially viable until coal was at least twice its current price.

The message from the McKinsey Curve was not that we lacked the technologies to solve climate change. The technologies were already here and they worked well. There were any number of ways to deliver reliable carbon-neutral electricity into our homes and offices. You could even get around the geography problem if you used batteries to store electricity from the good times.

The real problem, and the one that was hard for most people to see, was that these technologies were not getting the chance to move down the cost curve. Technologies could only become cheaper to produce if entrepreneurs were constantly working on them, monitoring the production process and refining the most expensive parts of the process. This required short-term investment for long-term reward. Instead, technologies were sitting unused in the garages of Silicon Valley entrepreneurs.

The challenge of cost-cutting was this. The best cost-cutting ideas came from experience rather than theory. Entrepreneurs did not sit around waiting for a brilliant idea to hit them. They were constantly tinkering with and perfecting their inventions. Without the initial seed capital, however, they were forced to fight a price war before they had even entered the market.

Contrary to Dean's price-maker strategy, clean-energy technologies were born into an environment where they were already price takers. Since many of these technologies never sold a single console, they didn't achieve the economies of scale and improvements which usually came from real life – what economists called "learning by doing". This wasn't a technical problem, it was an economic one. Because clean tech was competing in a distinctly low-tech environment, the traditional economics of innovation were being forced out of alignment.

4.

How to solve this problem? Did you need the government to intervene? And, if so, how would the intervention be framed to avoid market-wide distortions? When I put these thoughts to Timothy Draper, he was not convinced. Draper was a co-founder of Draper Fischer Jurvetson, one of the finest venture capital firms in Silicon Valley engaged in clean tech.

"Why do you think government has a role to play?" came his reply, moments after I had sent him an email. I wasn't sure that government did have a role to play but that was what I wanted to talk to him about, I wrote back.

"I don't have time to meet with a socialist like you," he replied. When it came to the unadulterated free market, Draper was the real McCoy. The DFJ website showed him riding a mechanical bull in his office. When he was invited to give Harvard MBAs career advice, he was famous for delivering a rap he wrote called "The Riskmaster". It was an ode to the entrepreneur who risks everything to bring to market a novel idea: "He's got a mission / Company vision / An artist's ambition / Gut intuition / Fearless and free employee / No guarantee for the corporate escapee ... He is the Riskmaster / Lives fast drives faster / Skates on the edge of disaster / He is the Riskmaster / To the moon!"

Despite appearances, though, Draper was a serious businessman. His cheques had helped start, among others, Skype and Hotmail – which, incidentally, credited him with inventing that form of viral marketing known as spam. But Draper was also a man in possession of an intellectual magnifying glass, one no less powerful than that wielded by the Malthusian or the person who stared at the weather. In Draper's worldview, the economy would solve climate change at its own pace and without any help.

There was much to admire in Draper's willingness to take risks and shape the future, but on the matter of clean technology the challenges ran much deeper. In theory the idea that the invisible hand would revolutionise the energy sector unassisted was right. In practice, though, it was suffering from a bout of arthritis.

I discussed this with Raj Atluru, who at the time headed Draper's clean-tech group. He was more sober about the barriers to clean-tech investment. That week, Atluru explained, the US Department of Energy had announced a US$535 million loan guarantee for Solyndra, a local solar company. It followed a similar US$250 million loan to Bright Source, another solar company, a few months earlier. Publicly, these loans were a response to the global financial crisis, but in the offices of Silicon Valley the word was that the government was trying to tackle the Valley of Death. It wasn't necessarily the right approach to take. Solyndra collapsed in late 2011 in spite of the government loan. But at least the government had begun to recognise the structural, uphill battle facing innovators of clean-energy technologies. The government loan wasn't targeted at the two barriers we have talked about so far: the small-market problem and the pricing conundrum. It was aimed at a third barrier: extraordinarily high start-up costs.

Most technology start-ups had relatively modest initial costs. Software companies, for example, needed just enough money early on to buy college kids pizza to eat while they wrote code over a summer. Healthcare products and drugs were relatively more expensive, but pharmaceutical companies typically had deep research and development budgets and an acute sense of when a drug trial had good prospects and when it needed to be switched off. By and large, the dynamics were entirely different in the energy sector.

In the first instance, energy companies typically dedicated a tiny fraction of their annual budget to research and development. They did not have the same culture of research as other technology-led companies. Secondly and more significantly, these costs were largely incurred by piloting a large piece of infrastructure, something which was inherently more expensive than demonstrating a small digital device.

A new wind-turbine facility could easily cost over US$100 million to test in a full demonstration plant and might take up to seven or eight years to come to fruition. The same could be said for large infrastructure-style projects

174

using technologies such as clean coal and hydrogen fuel cells. First Solar, the world's largest solar-power manufacturer, was a case in point. The company absorbed US$300 million of early-stage investment and it took over seven years of technological development before it sold its first product. The company was largely helped in this feat by one of the world's richest men, the late John Walton of the Wal-Mart fortune. Had it not been for Walton, venture capitalists may not have been as patient with the company. "We would have cut them off a long time ago," one of Atluru's colleagues told me frankly.

The problem with clean tech was that it was a large investment risk proportionate to the potential financial reward. The problem was not that venture capitalists did not have enough money. It was that they expected a greater return on the risk they were taking. If they had US$200 million under management, they preferred to split their investment across ten US$20 million investments, each of which had the opportunity to make a return. If one was spectacularly successful – what Atluru called an out-of-the-ballpark success – then the fund was handsomely rewarded for its risks. (Venture capitalists earned their living off these kinds of successes.) But if its funds were soaked up by two US$100 million investments, the chance of an out-of-the-ballpark success was significantly narrowed. "Capital intensity is the largest barrier," Derrick Lee from Bessemer Venture Partners explained. "When companies need to build a US$100 million facility, what they frankly need is project finance."

There were some in Silicon Valley who disputed this conclusion. Vinod Khosla, one of the Valley's wealthiest venture capitalists from the IT sector, argued that the problem with the clean-tech sector was that investors refused to show enough courage. By his reckoning, capital intensity was not really a barrier to investment; you just had to raise bigger pots of dough. But as I took my conversations from Silicon Valley back across the Atlantic to London and Oxford, venture capitalists in Europe expressed a similar view to Atluru and Lee's. The economics of clean tech were out of alignment, they told me, but explaining why ran counter to most people's image of how markets worked.

5.

It was theoretically possible to push these hurdles aside. However, the country that was most successful at doing so was not necessarily the one whose overall economic policies you would want to emulate. Nor was it the place most people thought of when you said the words "climate change" and "market economy". A highly flexible workforce, engineering endeavour, combined with sheer brute force had allowed it to do things that were not always possible in a free market.

China was an ambiguous role model for entrepreneurship. Its reputation in the international media was as the last post of state-centred socialism. Ever since Mao, the Chinese Communist Party had issued five-year plans which moved the economy forward one jolt at a time. But the country's rapid ascent was forcing its leaders to rethink their strategy. China could not stay a sweatshop for low-end manufacturing forever. If it was to pull its workers out of poverty and continue to grow, it needed to graduate to a high value-adding economy.

China's ambition to do something on climate change should not be underestimated. In early 2010, shortly after the world negotiated the Copenhagen Accord, the premier of China, Wen Jiabao, invited the country's top industrialists and party officials to a conference call. China fully intended to fulfil its commitments under the Copenhagen agreement, he told them. The responsibility now lay with them to fully implement their commitments. He didn't care what they did or how they did it. All that mattered was that goals were achieved. If they met their individual commitments, they would be promoted. If they failed, they would be sacked.

One of China's most successful climate capitalists was Shi Zhengrong. Shi was more than familiar with the downside of socialism. In the 1960s his parents had found themselves left behind in Mao's Great Leap Forward. Shi was born the younger of twins. Since his parents were too poor to support an extra child, they gave Shi up for adoption to a couple who had suffered a stillbirth that same morning.

Shi excelled through school, then university. In the late '80s he migrated to Australia just as his country became engulfed in the events of Tiananmen Square. Shi earned his doctorate in solar engineering and was soon working for a start-up in Sydney called Pacific Solar. By the late '90s he was contemplating a change. Pacific Solar needed more cash and it was struggling to cut its production costs in Australia.

In early 2000, four officials from Wuxi City in China flew out to Australia to make Shi an offer. Return to China, they said, and they would help him enter business for himself. He would get cheap land, dexterous labour and a US$6 million equity investment. He eventually agreed and the Wuxi Suntech Power Corporation was incorporated with the local state-owned enterprise in late 2001. Within five years it had listed on the New York Stock Exchange, raising close to US$400 million on its debut.

The Suntech story proved that costs could be cut when the right business model was applied. Shi's invention was not in intellectual property. The design for his solar panel was based on a patent from the space race which had recently expired. His real innovation was to decentralise the process of manufacturing solar panels. Decentralisation was a counter-intuitive process to apply in the manufacturing industry. Centralisation was far more common in places like Germany and the United States. Q-Cells, Suntech's main German rival, for example, prided itself on its high-tech robots, which were able to do a single, centrally programmable task faster than any human on earth. The problem with automation, though, was that it came at the cost of flexibility.

By replacing robots with the hands of Chinese workers, Shi's strategy was to de-automate the layering of silicon onto solar panels. That part of the manufacturing process had always been the trickiest and most expensive. De-automation gave Shi more room to experiment with how silicon could be applied. Whereas it took Q-Cells a week to reorganise its chain of production, Suntech could make the change in a few hours by shuffling its workers around. The result revolutionised the cost of making solar panels. When he had pitched his company to the Wuxi municipal government in 2001, Shi had promised to take the cost of solar from US$5 a watt to US$3 a watt in two years – an unimaginable achievement. By late 2003 he was generating electricity for US$2.80 a watt at a gross profit margin of 25 per cent.

A decentralised approach to high-tech manufacturing was part of what the *Economist* called "frugal innovation". The term referred to the ability of developing countries to invert the traditional economics of innovation. Whereas the rich world had once built the computers and the poor world had made the cardboard boxes, frugal innovation was the ability to apply low-cost manufacturing to high-end goods. Frugal innovation helped with clean tech's invisible barriers in two respects. First, it went some way to reducing the high upfront costs of projects. Secondly, it drove clean-electricity prices to convergence with the fossil-fuel economy. Geography was a more difficult problem to solve. However, batteries helped address one piece of this puzzle: the sporadic nature of renewable energy generation. If renewable electricity could be stored in batteries over the long haul, then the fickleness of the weather became less of a problem.

One Chinese entrepreneur who had applied frugal innovation to batteries was Wang Chuan-Fu, the founder of China's largest battery manufacturer, BYD. Over the company's first ten years Wang had taken the cost of a lithium ion battery from US$40 to US$12. This feat was achieved by replacing machines with workers. Chinese industrialists had previously avoided this strategy because it was thought to introduce too much human error into high-tech manufacturing. Wang proved that with training and the right procedures you could overcome the problem. The result not only had the potential to change the world's auto industries, it might also save the world. Lithium ion batteries were the rechargeable power behind the modern electric car.

On a recent trip to the United States Wang had disappeared for a time, only to be found under the bonnet of one of the cars in his entourage. He had been trying to work out how American engines were put together. When he had brought out the prototypes for his first low-cost hybrid and electric cars in the mid 2000s, the automobile executives from Detroit had laughed at him. By the time he released his first mass-produced line a few years later, even Warren Buffett was queuing up for a chance to invest in his company.

China was not only changing the cost structure of high-tech goods. It was changing the way it acquired intellectual property. Ideas were no longer flowing from Europe down to Asia. Open-source networks were spreading ideas across a more even surface. This was known as "polycentric innovation". China was capitalising on the footloose habits of the modern corporate executive, willing to flirt with one company and then plant themselves inside another. The effect was to change the geography of where innovation took place. "In the 20th Century, enterprises satisfied their innovation needs largely through their own in-house R&D

programs," Francis Gurry, the head of the World Intellectual Property Organization, said in late 2009. "In the 21st Century, more and more enterprises are seeking to answer their innovation needs also through collaboration with other enterprises and institutions."

One of the best examples of this was in China's wind-power industry. Throughout the 1980s and '90s, China's largest wind company, Goldwind, had featured at the low-tech end of several wind-power deals in China. By the early 2000s it was making a conscious effort to reposition itself in the market closer to the intellectual property. Since so many of the best engineering ideas in wind technology had traditionally come from Germany, Denmark or the United States, Chinese companies sent their employees on tours for advanced training. Goldwind set up direct partnerships with two European companies in the sector, REpower and Vensys. The partnerships allowed Chinese engineers to travel to Europe and learn how to design wind turbines from scratch. In exchange the Chinese offered the Europeans low-cost manufacturing.

In 2008, once Goldwind had acquired all the skills and the experience it needed, it raised €41 million to buy a 70 per cent stake in Vensys. The deal gave Goldwind exclusive rights to Vensys's intellectual property and allowed it to leapfrog its way to international leadership in the sector far quicker than if it had developed its own intellectual property from scratch. The pattern has been mimicked by almost every Chinese clean-tech success including Sinovel (another wind producer), as well as BYD and Suntech Power.

6.

We have been accustomed to thinking that high-tech innovation flows in a predictable direction. Rich places like the United States and Europe own the intellectual property. Countries like China and India are mainly used for cheap manufacturing. The truth, though, is that forces are at work to invert the usual order of things.

The success of China's clean-tech industry showed how the global economy was changing. While entrepreneurs in the United States and Europe sat in the Valley of Death, the Chinese were becoming billionaires. China's success posed a challenge to other economies. How did you compete with a country whose government was the venture capitalist of first resort?

There were two ways of responding. One was to try and compete with China's brute force. This approach argued for a big, interventionist government. If only the government had more skin in the game, then domestic businesses would have better prospects. In other words, a more centrally minded government was the only way forward.

The alternative and opposite idea was that the government needed to step away completely. Maybe Timothy Draper was right. There was nothing the government could do which the market couldn't do better.

Yet there was also a third option, one which took the traditional distinction between big and small government and reframed it. It was much better to find a path between the two positions: for a government to breathe life into the *spirit* of entrepreneurial capitalism. This required introducing correct incentives and giving entrepreneurs a better chance of reaching their potential. It was a messier process but one more in tune with the economy's inherent complexity.

Another way of putting it was this. Although "frugal innovation" was unique to developing countries, its instincts were universal. Ideas flourished when power was decentralised. The early stages of invention were improved by flexibility rather than by automation. Workers were more productive when they were given more responsibility, not less. And people were at their most creative when they were free to work open-source.

Decentralising power was a wonderful way of running a start-up business. It also made a lot of sense in the case of public administration. The best type of government was arguably not the one that solved problems for entrepreneurial people. It was the one that found ways to help entrepreneurial people solve problems themselves.

CHAPTER 8

HEDGEHOG VERSUS FOX

why nimble is better

In the mid 2000s Mark Martinez faced an unusual problem. Martinez was a manager at Southern California Edison, California's local electricity supplier. He had been given the task of getting customers to curb their electricity use. It seemed strange that an electricity company would want to reduce its customers' usage, but what they really wanted was to shift the way customers consumed electricity. Coal-fired power stations were not built with an on-off switch. You had to run them night and day at a level which met peak demand, which in most places was around 6 p.m., when people came home from work and cooked dinner. If Southern California Edison could get its customers to switch some of their household chores to off-peak times, then the company could save money. Not only could it stoke its power plants with less coal, it could substantially reduce the tonnage of carbon emissions entering the atmosphere.

Martinez's early strategies had failed – automated emails, text messages and reminder phone calls. Then he hit upon the Ambient Orb. The Orb was a desktop device which you put on the kitchen table, where it glowed either red or green. Red indicated the electricity grid was going through a peak zone. Green meant there were fewer users on the system. Martinez sent 120 Orbs to Edison customers and monitored their electricity usage. What he discovered was astonishing.

Within a few weeks, Orb users had dramatically cut their electricity consumption. Every time the Orb glowed red, people ran around their house switching off lights and devices which weren't needed. When the Orb was green, people headed to their laundries to do an extra load of washing. The numbers which arrived on Martinez's desk from the trial were striking: peak usage was down 40 per cent, and non-essential consumption fell sharply.

The Ambient Orb had uncovered the real reason people struggled to change their behaviour. It wasn't that they didn't care about the environment or saving money. It was that they struggled to get the information they needed to make a difference. "Electricity is invisible," Clive Thompson wrote in *Wired* magazine about Martinez's discovery. By feeding real-time information about electricity usage to ordinary households he had found a way of helping them see the world.

Martinez's approach to enabling change was not an isolated one; similar ideas could be seen in entirely different parts of society. Doctors were transforming the delivery of health services to diabetics by giving them devices to self-manage their care. (This allowed patients to do things which previously required a suite of hospital staff.) And information disclosure through tools like crowd-sourcing was transforming everything from restaurant hygiene to the way we donated to charities. If there was a larger principle behind what Martinez had uncovered, it had to do with the mechanism powering society's problem-solving brain. Our best decisions did not come from dictates delivered from the top down. They came from initiatives carried out from the bottom up.

There had long been a view that big, collective-action problems were best solved from the commanding heights. The average citizen was either too simple or too selfish to tackle the big issues. We needed intelligent bureaucrats to solve our trickiest dilemmas from on high. But an alternative view said that this was to undervalue ordinary people. People were actually surprisingly *good* at organising themselves. Most had good hearts and wanted a better future. The greatest challenges were not ones of intention, but ones of execution and information. In the fight for a better world, where did you start?

Localism argued that execution started with the close at hand. Big problems were best solved locally, not because magnificent, top-down leaders weren't important, but because our fellow citizens were most moved by what they saw in the person next to them. Society moved forward by the effort of little platoons. There was a method to how these platoons coordinated their activities. What gave localism its connecting thread was not government – bureaucrats, politicians, international agreements and directives. It was information – the internet, word of mouth, stories and rumour.

It could be a messy way of working, but localism placed faith in the view that, when presented with the best answers, people had the intelligence to spot them. It took time, patience and a lot of experimentation. We had to try many strategies before we found the one that worked. When we unearthed it, though, it caught on quickly. It was too easy to fixate on the notion that the world's fight was fought by generals: that was the magnifying glass trap with government. What it missed were the more powerful forces changing society from the bottom up.

1.

Garrett Hardin, the Malthusian scientist we met earlier, was a firm holder of the first view of human society. When he wrote "The Tragedy of the Commons" in 1968, he painted a gloomy, doom-struck picture of the world. Our cities were overcrowded, our resources were dwindling. Sooner or later the planet would become a wasteland. Solving these problems came down to faith in one thing, he said: top-down government. "People must be responsive to a coercive force outside their individual psyches, a 'Leviathan', to use Hobbes's term," he later wrote.

Top-down government was a conceptually intoxicating idea. In the presence of uncertainty, we tended to reach for comforting answers rather than giving new things a go. Tversky and Kahneman described this quality as ambiguity aversion – our dislike for what was unclear. It often led us to jump to conclusions before the best answers surfaced. The Leviathan neatly fed this emotion. It constructed an artificial, abstract entity – commanding government – to save us from our woe and ignorance.

Hardin's pessimism was encapsulated in a neat logical puzzle. Imagine a grazing pasture freely open to any shepherd who passed by. To those transfixed by higher authority, the result of this scenario was *always* the same. A rational shepherd added more and more sheep to the land because he incurred a benefit without bearing a cost. As other herders did the same, the pasture would be destroyed. "Ruin is the destination toward which all men rush, each pursuing his own best interest in a society that believes in the freedom of the commons," Hardin mused.

If Hardin was always right, then that would have ended the matter. We would all yield to the embrace of top-down government. There were many examples where Hardin *was* right, of course. But a too-heavy reliance on this view could also miss something essential about human society. Hardin had assumed in his puzzle that shepherds did not talk to each other. They operated in a vacuum of mechanical self-interest. In reality, of course, people lived in lively local communities. When you adjusted for this fact, history threw up some surprising results.

One academic who had done more than most to unlock the tragedy of the commons was the American political scientist Elinor Ostrom. In 1990 she had published a book called *Governing the Commons*, in which she brought a new subtlety to the debate. Free market fundamentalists and top-down bureaucratic zealots were guilty of the same mistake. They fixated on an abstract idea and they missed the complexity of how society solved problems. "Instead of there being a single solution to a single problem," she argued, the answers varied according to local conditions.

People in other words – busy, talkative, reflective and self-questioning – were best at solving big problems. With one ear to the ground, they often had a better sense of what was missing than did the cold eye of government. Yet to encourage people to believe in their own problem-solving ability was no easy task. People had been lectured about their inadequacies and moral turpitude for centuries. You also needed certain other conditions for community localism to work: a common language, social relationships, good information and democratic freedoms. But the bigger point was this: placing faith in ordinary people often solved our bigger and messier problems more reliably than delegating to distant authority.

Having faith that big problems could be solved by small communities was such a paradoxical and controversial idea that Ostrom won the 2009 Nobel Prize in Economics for expressing it. Her argument was built on hundreds of case studies where she had found local communities solving enormous problems with nuanced, cooperative answers. At first, these solutions seemed lucky – random moments of social genius with no guarantee that they would be repeated for other problems or in other times or places. On closer inspection, though, she realised that while the answers changed, the process to reach them was often the same.

Answers evolved by way of a slow, incremental process which fashioned and refashioned the answer until the puzzle was eventually unlocked. It was evolutionary biology at work in a human geography. One of the most intriguing examples of this had been in Alanya, a remote fishing village in the south of Turkey.

Alanya's local fishing community had been devastated by open competition. Neighbouring fishermen had hounded their shores, driving fish stocks down and impoverishing local families. The natural instinct of the community to solve this problem might have been to turn to the Turkish government, which could have banned new fishermen or limited access to particular fishing sites. Instead, in the late 1970s, the members of the local collective devised a scheme to introduce more information into Alanya's fishing market.

One of the problems of over-fishing had been that there were no visible borders between high- and low-yield fishing sites. Using ancient knowledge, the collective divided their fishery into zones and held a lottery which allocated the different zones to interested fishermen each year. From September to January, each fisherman moved east each day to fish at the next location on the map. From January to May, they then moved back west. The arrangement gave each fisherman an equal right to fish across the water. It was also self-enforcing because everyone had the same interest in not usurping their neighbours' interests.

A key ingredient in the scheme's success was the local information which led to the creation of the fishing map. This information had been previously invisible to fishermen entering Alanya from neighbouring areas, and the result had been chaos. By making this world transparent, it re-instilled order in the community. Ostrom argued that bureaucrats working from on high could not have discerned this kind of detailed information. "Central-government officials could not have crafted such a set of rules without assigning a full-time staff to work (actually fish) in the area for an extended period," she wrote. In the end, infractions ended and fishing stocks recovered. The story disproved the common wisdom that "left to their own devices, fishermen will overexploit stocks," and "to avoid disaster, managers must have effective hegemony over them," she wrote.

Ostrom had revealed a world which had been hitherto overlooked by many cynics and pessimists. They had long assumed that problems of collective action could only be solved when a manager passed Resolution X. Resolution X was a grand statement of what *had* to be done. For Ostrom, though, the best answers came from bringing into the open the information which others had missed.

Bottom-up governance was a difficult, time-consuming and conflict-provoking process. It involved adapting to local conditions and shuffling the pieces until the best answers fitted together. But this kind of experimentation – this social entrepreneurship – was no different, in practice, to Shi Zhengrong's improvisation with solar-power manufacturing or Wang Chuan-Fu's disassembling of the lithium ion battery. "The centrists presume that unified authorities will operate in the field as they have been designed to do in the textbooks," Ostrom wrote. In practice, the world progressed by a process of trial and error.

2.

Localism was a new way of thinking about global problems. Lowering a single template on the globe would have been a brilliant idea if everyone agreed with one another. It appeared to have a number of pluses: simplicity, coherence, control and uniformity. It was especially gratifying if you sat at the helm. But the alternative view simply noted that the world was too diverse for everyone to agree. In any case, simple, coherent and surprisingly uniform solutions were most reliably unearthed when we placed faith in the genius of local communities.

People had a kind of in-built homing device when it came to good ideas. When local communities were allowed to experiment *and* the information about their answers was freely traded, people were extremely good at copying the best answers and discarding the rest. The world was held together by social networks.

Consider the conduct of international affairs. Diplomats had long witnessed how fiercely states argued over collective-action problems. The nuclear arms build-up had kept the world on edge during the Cold War, and the hole in the ozone layer caused friction in the late 1980s and '90s. However, neither of these problems surpassed climate change in complexity and collective disagreement. The arms build-up, for example, only involved two nations – the Soviet Union and the United States. And ozone-depleting gases had had relatively cheap substitutes. With climate change, not only did some people disagree that it was even a problem, many also disagreed on how to solve it.

When Wen Jiabao, the Chinese premier, arrived at the international climate change negotiations in Copenhagen in December 2009, he found his country under severe attack. Many in the media and elsewhere had accused China of defaulting on its civic obligations. The strongest attacks came from the newly elected president of the United States. On the last day of the conference, Barack Obama had flown in from Washington DC to give the lunchtime talk at the Bella Centre. "As the world's largest economy and as the world's *second* largest emitter," he said, "America bears our responsibility to address climate change, and we intend to meet that responsibility."

As the translation came through on their headsets, most of the Chinese delegation stood up and left for the airport. China was the world's largest emitter and the implication of the president's speech was that China was not fulfilling its responsibility. China's critics misunderstood the country's complex position. China was prepared to transform its energy sector, a negotiator later told me. The challenge was balancing poverty alleviation against costly reforms. The two goals could be achieved, but this required some improvisation. Putting the country in a straitjacket and slowly tightening the straps was no way of encouraging international compliance.

Obama's lunchtime remarks had turned out to be counterproductive. At a 2 p.m. meeting scheduled between the two countries, the president found himself sitting across the table from Ye Hafei, China's vice foreign minister. When he realised he was being stonewalled by a middling official,

Obama stood up and left. The leaders of Europe, Australia and Canada got the same treatment later that afternoon. "Why can't we even mention our targets?" yelled a furious German chancellor to a row of Chinese delegates.

Around 5 p.m., the US presidential advisers received a call. Premier Wen was willing to meet with the president and his secretary of state if they reconsidered their position. They agreed, and a back room of the Bella Centre was set aside for a 7 p.m. meeting. When the two American leaders arrived, they found the Chinese premier chairing a meeting with the leaders of Brazil, India and South Africa. Obama pulled up a seat next to President Lula of Brazil, the doors shut, and the negotiations began.

The Copenhagen Accord was negotiated in two hours and was only two pages long. It reversed the governing logic of the Kyoto Protocol. The Kyoto Protocol was a top-down agreement. It had been invented by the Europeans in the late '90s to divide the world in two zones – developed and developing nations – and institute a series of targets and timelines handed down from above. But a punishing regime of top-down targets only worked for simple problems like schoolyard discipline. When you added more complexity to the problem, it became too difficult to control. The inevitable result was that, instead of getting the best out of each participant, the collective target drifted towards the lowest common denominator. Even Anthony Giddens, the British sociologist who had once advised British prime minister Tony Blair on his "Third Way" politics, admitted the limits to centrally planning the global economy. "It will not be through Kyoto-style agreement that most progress will be made," he wrote in his 2009 book *The Politics of Climate Change*.

The new Copenhagen Accord worked by the opposite principle – by devolving power to states. Countries made pledges on what they could do and they were held to their word by information disclosure and international monitoring. The Accord settled on a general objective to limit the planet's temperature to two degrees of warming, but how this was achieved was left to domestic legislatures to decide. Critics lamented the lack of centralised control in the Accord, but its efficacy must ultimately be proved in practice.

"Although the Copenhagen Accord has been criticised by some as inadequate or worse, it represents a potentially significant breakthrough," wrote Professor Dan Bodansky, who had tracked the negotiations, several months later. Not only had sixty-seven nations representing 80 per cent of the world's global greenhouse gases signed up to the Accord within its first three months. (The Kyoto Protocol had been signed by about 180 nations, but covered only about 65 per cent of emissions.) According to a UN Environment Programme report published one year later, the voluntary pledges by the Accord's early adopters went up to 60 per cent of the way towards the final two degrees target. More action was needed, but it was a promising start.

If the Copenhagen Accord indeed worked (and it was too early to pass definitive judgement), it would be for the same reason that Alanya had been able to fix its fisheries and Martinez to change electricity consumption: it trusted in the ability of local actors to achieve results. Signatories to the Copenhagen Accord did not reach their ends by altruism. Countries, like people, were competitive, ambitious and socially self-conscious. What allowed them to compete with each other was information. When everyone knew what everyone else was doing, rivalry and accountability in the world of public affairs ensued. In the eighteenth century, Jeremy Bentham had invented the panopticon, a prison where all the inmates faced a central tower staffed by unseen guards. It engendered a constant fear in the inmates that the guards were watching them. The Copenhagen Accord was like the panopticon of international affairs. It held nations to account by the ceaseless gaze of onlookers – in this case, other countries.

It wasn't just the environment for which bottom-up governance was making a big difference: take any problem that was socially messy or complicated and the devolution of power changed how well you could solve it. Another case in point was the fight against global poverty. It was one thing to campaign for more foreign-aid funding at the elite govern-ment level. The UN Millennium Project, for example, had sought to increase government donations to 0.7 per cent of their Gross National Product. But the more complex question was how to best deliver that money to actually alleviate poverty. Increasing government aid was important, but it was how you spent the money that made the biggest difference to poverty, and here localism also had an essential role to play.

In 1989, Porto Alegre, one of Brazil's largest cities, had experimented with the idea that people, rather than govern-ments, were better at deciding where their tax dollars went.

The country had suffered two decades of dictatorship and a newly elected local government wanted to experiment with "participatory budgeting". The challenge was whether people could be trusted with common pools of resources (the local government budget) or whether they were more likely to siphon these off for private ends or just spend them foolishly.

When the project started, most Brazilians in Porto Alegre lived in slum housing. The streets were unpaved and the public squares dotted with sewage. Participatory budgeting tackled this problem a bit like speed dating. Locals were invited to attend town-hall meetings where series of spending options were proposed. Participants, divided into their localities, then whittled them away to a shortlist. That shortlist was weighted according to various metrics and given a final score. The top-scoring projects were funded by the government and the mayor only vetoed them in exceptional circumstances.

The results were remarkable. Not only did tax evasion in the city decrease, but the number of households with sewer and water connections went from 75 per cent to 98 per cent over the decade, and the number of schools quadrupled over the same period. Progress was faster than in other districts which resorted to traditional bureaucracy. The process worked because locals understood their own needs better than bureaucrats with a clipboard surveying the area on a day visit. Things which bureaucrats struggled to observe would quickly register in the participant budgeting. Locals also felt more engaged in the world, and the number of attendees at meetings soon grew.

Participatory budgeting was not confined to the world of the poor. As Britain languished in political stasis through the early 2000s, local councils experimented with a similar idea. In the London borough of Tower Hamlets, the organisers of "You Decide!" coordinated participatory budgeting for £2.4 million in projects. Participants were equipped with keypads – like those on *Who Wants To Be a Millionaire?* – and asked to state their preferences. At the end of the process, most participants said they would do it again.

Faith in the bottom-up mechanism of social change also worked in education. When a conservative coalition government was elected in Britain in 2010, one of the biggest reforms on its agenda was the introduction of charter schools into the country.

Charter schools (also known as free schools) gave parents and teachers more say in the way their local school was run. Their benefit was customisation: the ability to tailor education to the needs of the students. If students in the local area had poor literacy rates, for example, you could add extra classes to the curriculum. If parents wanted their children to play sport or learn a musical instrument, there were ways of adding these to the program. In a centrally planned system, there was less room to manoeuvre, though it offered more predictability and control.

Critics of a British charter school system argued that it added *too* much variety. "There will be no planning at all. It will just be up to groups of parents," Polly Toynbee from the *Guardian* said in a debate against Toby Young from the *Spectator*. Further, the kind of variety it added to society was not the sort Toynbee wanted. "Every single church will have the ability, if they want, to say: 'we want another school here' ... This is a recipe for chaos."

Yet in a sense variety was the whole point. By dissolving the top-down managerial template, the newly elected government was trying to cater for the nuances of the population. Well-meaning bureaucrats inside airless offices could rarely see what was happening on the ground, and their instincts often flattened creativity. There were limits to localism, of course. Schools still needed to meet basic education standards and the government would guarantee public funding. But in its own chaotic and uncoordinated way this approach had the capacity to lift standards for all.

Grounds for such optimism came from the United States, where the idea had already been tested. When it had first been introduced two decades earlier, critics had been afraid of private forces. Charter schools were often run by social entrepreneurs who received funding from the government for their services. They were not allowed to charge students for their tuition, but the schools were shaped from the bottom up by the local preferences of parents and educators. By 2009, 4700 charter schools had spawned across America educating over 1.4 million children, with more than 365,000 names on waiting lists.

New Orleans provided an event study on how charter schools could transform struggling areas. Before the city was struck by Hurricane Katrina in 2005, only 2 per cent of schools in the city were organised by charter. The Orleans parish had terrible educational results for children.

The parish ranked sixty-seventh out of sixty-eight for student performance across Louisiana state, and Louisiana ranked somewhere between forty-third and forty-sixth on the federal government's state rankings. According to the state's accountability statistics for 2004, two-thirds of Orleans students, mainly black, were "failing".

The state legislature had created a Recovery School District to kickstart improvement in underprivileged schools, but at the time of the hurricane only five schools had been converted to charter. In November 2005, the legislature held a special session to convert a further 107 schools (covering 60 per cent of the city's students) to charter. The results were striking. By the 2010–11 academic year the number of students failing in the Orleans parish was down to less than a third. This meant there was a lot more to do, but as Leslie Jacobs, a local education advocate, told *Newsweek*, "the fact that we haven't got everything right yet shouldn't take away from the fact that we're getting a whole lot more right."

Charter schools improved the quality of education a student received for a simple reason. There was more transparency and accountability about how a school was run. Teachers shared more information with parents about how their children were faring, and parents could hold teachers to account if their classes didn't work. In one case, Ben Marcovitz, the CEO of Sci Academy, had opened a high school in New Orleans where he taught the standard freshman curriculum: one period of English, one period of mathematics, and so on. However, he quickly learnt that most students in the area had below-average literacy. He responded with an extra dose of literacy courses to get students up to speed, changing the entire curriculum over a weekend. It was an extreme scenario, but it was only possible because of the new flexibility in the school system.

Charter schools were not the panacea to education reform. You had to be careful about replacing the top-down magnifying glass with an equally strong bottom-up one. In 2009, for example, a critical report published by Stanford University argued that educators were better at starting charter schools than they were at shutting down bad ones. But the most important insight in bottom-up governance was that you had to enter the problem at the right level in order to solve it.

Experimentation was part of the localism phenomenon. It did not arrive at the best answers by pursuing its own fix-ations. Its philosophy, by nature, was dynamic and cre-ative. Schools hit upon successful ideas by copying what worked elsewhere and changing those things which were least successful in the local setting. For this to happen, the community needed to be flush with information. When one charter school hit upon a successful idea, word trav-elled fast and others followed. When another school lagged its peers, Facebook groups were set up to persuade school principals to conduct a review. Improving education was no different to alleviating poverty or taming climate change: the mechanics for change often came from the social guerillas on the ground, rather than generals on their commandeering heights.

3.

Localism did for government what the internet had done for knowledge. It opened us up to things we never knew existed. When we relied on a single institution or individual to solve our problems, the answers were often a poor fit with reality. The great quirk of history was that small answers were the best way of solving big problems.

In 1953, the philosopher Isaiah Berlin wrote an essay which developed this point. The essay moved beyond the humdrum consideration of worldly problems to make a comment about human history. It opened with a fragment from the ancient Greek poet Archilochus: "The fox knows many things, but the hedgehog knows one big thing." No one was quite sure what Archilochus had meant, but in *The Hedgehog and the Fox* Berlin offered his own interpretation.

The world was divided into two kinds of people, Berlin wrote. Hedgehogs were those in possession of a single, unifying idea. They insisted our best answers came from feeding things through a central prism, "a single, central vision, one system, less or more coherent". In the context of this book, they were the ones gripping the magnifying glass tightly.

The other sort of person – the fox – was more agile in their approach. They sought to improve the world by constantly shifting their perspective on it. They saw the many different ways to solve a particular problem, and constantly adjusted their focus until the best answers came into view. The fox would "pursue many ends, often unrelated and even contradictory", he wrote, less inclined to universal answers and more adept at fitting the circumstances.

Foxes and hedgehogs were not necessarily unchanging human types. They could also be choices we made about how we planned for the future. A hedgehog could become more fox-like if he became aware of his own magnifying glass. A fox could become more hedgehog-like if they became too dogmatic in their view of the world. What kept the spirit of the fox alive was their self-doubt. The fox was never certain they had the right answer and so was constantly unfulfilled, searching for a better one. Hedgehogs, the psychologist Philip Tetlock later argued, usually thought that they were right about things. Foxes always doubted themselves, but their answers often turned out to be better.

In my last year at Oxford, I flew to New York for a wedding where I met someone who taught me this lesson. His name was Paul Sperduto and he was the proprietor of Moon River Chattel. One evening while visiting the future bride and groom, I commented on the beautiful things in their house. Many were from Sperduto's shop, they told me. In the '90s, Sperduto had worked as a property developer on Manhattan Island, New York, stripping old buildings and preparing them for demolition. But one day, as he stared at a magnificent old hotel in mid-town, he decided it was time to change his career. Paul Sperduto's products had slowly made their way around Brooklyn, but what fascinated me was how his philosophy had travelled with them.

Sperduto had set up Moon River Chattel in Williamsburg, a post-industrial suburb on the rough side of Brooklyn. The shop took the fixtures and fittings of disused buildings and sold them to anyone who was interested. At first his customers were artists and the destitute. But as the tech bubble burst, his shop filled up with a different kind of customer: lawyers, bankers and ex-IT executives, all seeking a simpler life.

Sperduto was an intriguing figure to me. He was clearly intelligent and very well educated, but when I asked him what motivated him, he was rather vague. In the '90s he had been motivated by heritage conservation. He was shocked by the way buildings were torn down without regard for their history. By the 2000s he had adjusted his focus to rebuilding the local community. When he had first arrived in Williams- burg, the place was falling apart. Dealers traded crack on his corner and prostitutes strutted the street. He had fixed up his shop and helped open a local school. As people returned to the area, new services began to appear. They were thinking of issuing their own merchant scrip, he told me. It would be a currency to bring local businesses together.

It struck me that Sperduto was a man wrestling with globalisation. The problems he wanted to solve were exam- ples of urban blight. You could see the same trend in Baltimore and Detroit. The harsh edge of capitalism had wiped out whole industries, leaving in their wake empty buildings and crime.

But Sperduto's approach to solving things did not fall under any easy label. He wasn't a pure capitalist, because he was unsettled by radical change. Nor was he a socialist, because he held governments in low esteem. He had tried to start some initiatives with them, but none had been very fruitful. "I try to ignore them as much as possible," he told me when I pressed him on the point.

Instead, Sperduto was a fixer. He muddled along as best he could. He solved problems with the tools he had, and when he realised he had missed something important, he would change tack. I walked away from my conversation with him feeling he had touched on something profound – I just couldn't quite work out what.

Perhaps it was the modesty he had brought to fighting the world's fights. Sperduto was not a distinguished statesman or captain of industry – no high-flier at all. Few people had heard of his little company in Brooklyn and no one recognised his face on the street. Yet when you spoke to the man and saw what he was doing, he was changing the world one project at a time. If it worked, someone else tried the same thing. And if both projects worked, they might take over the next neighbourhood, or maybe even the country, one day.

Paul Sperduto hadn't uncovered the answer to the world's biggest problems, I realised later. He had discovered the method. The world wasn't made better by singular answers. It was enriched by a process of experiment. We improved by tinkering, taking the wisdom of the past and changing what was least successful. As a fixer – caught between conserving heritage and inventing something new in his community – Sperduto had hit upon something most people missed. It was an unassuming way of changing the world. But to my mind at least, that made it all the more powerful.

CHANGING THE WORLD

one frame at a time

Several years after I returned from Costa Rica I found myself in a little convent alongside the Yarra River in Melbourne. It was summer and the heat was unbearable. A ceiling fan swept hot air around the room and fifty of us, all young, idealistic and ambitious, lay on our backs and closed our eyes. The session was on "future action" and a middle-aged woman, hired to moderate the session, tiptoed among us. "I want you to imagine your ideal future – what it would look like, feel like, smell like," she said.

We had travelled to Melbourne with a grand mission in mind – to set up the country's first youth group for climate change action. I had raised the money and a friend had invited the guests, but as the session wore on I became more and more troubled. "The end of capitalism," came a voice from the corner. "We need to put a stop to globalisation," said another. As the room filled up, I sat up and went outside.

There was something admirable about the people in the convent. They had big hearts and wanted a better world. But their way of changing it seemed odd to me. I was quick to admit that the planet wasn't perfect. You didn't have to be Mother Teresa to realise that there was intolerable injustice and poverty in the world. Only a true fatalist would argue that there were *no* grounds for change. But once you accepted that we needed to work for a better world, the question you had to ask yourself was how exactly you would achieve it. Did we need a clean sweep or something different?

Those in the convent felt an urgent need to de-industrialise the world. Many were still fired up from an anti-G20 rally, protesting against the economies which commanded world trade. It was one thing to argue that we had to change the world for the better. But to refashion it according to an abstract idea seemed to me an equal-but-opposite mistake to the one made by the person who wanted no change. One pointed to an impossible future, the other to an idealised freeze-frame. Like Berlin's hedgehogs, they filtered the world through a single prism and were dangerously oblivious to everything else around it.

Maybe there was a more reliable way to change the world – one which adjusted to find the best answers as they came in view. This alternative approach injected some modesty into universalising vistas. It accepted that society was unfathomably complex – far too complex to be grasped by even the most intelligent person on their own. Changing the world did not require the pursuit of a single idea or an over-arching theory but the ability to adapt. To arrive at our best answers we had first to put down the magnifying glass and engage with the part of the world where we lived.

Shortly after my Melbourne encounter I boarded a plane for Oxford. I spent the next few years trying to make sense of the clash I had felt. Could you reconcile economic growth with environmental sustainability? Was free-market capitalism incompatible with a more just world? Each year I spent at Oxford helped me to uncover a different piece of this puzzle. Much of what I learnt wasn't written down in books. It was discovered while sitting on a train to London, or on a trip through Silicon Valley, venturing inside the grand Parisian halls of the OECD or on the phone to Afghanistan. Life was awkward in that way. What looked good on paper didn't always make sense in practice.

The doctorate I eventually completed read nothing like this book. It was written in straight lines, and on the day I handed it in to the Bodleian Library in Oxford my entire body shook. I was worried about leaving the world of clean ideas, but in doing so I understood that I was accepting a new challenge.

This has been a book about vision. We have investigated the many ways we can look at the complex world around us but miss the deeper issues in play. We are attracted to microcosms – little pockets of certainty – which mask larger uncertainties. Recall, for example, the story of Merton and Scholes – the two giant brains powering Long-Term Capital Management. They lost billions by viewing the world through a peephole. Had they widened their gaze, they might have seen what was coming. Then there was the story of how the US military entered Iraq. The marines were trained to shoot insurgents, but they missed the insurgency. Had they tackled the grievances of restless Arab tribesmen, the war in Iraq might have subsided much sooner. You can switch the problem – from war, finance, the environment, immigration – and still make the same mistake.

Several years after the surge in Iraq, I asked John Nagl how he knew that he was right about flipping the way we saw terrorism.

"I didn't," the retired lieutenant colonel told me. "If we had failed in Iraq, we wouldn't be talking about counter-insurgency theory today."

Nagl had served during the Iraq invasion and helped to author the US military's new intellectual guidebook for fighting insurgencies. His answer surprised me at first, but on reflection it made sense. Experience, he said, was the best test of truth. If counterinsurgency had not worked, then the US military would have tried a different approach. The thing about counterinsurgency was that it was all about learning: "The side that learns fastest is the side that wins." His point was that the best solutions were rarely abstract ideas. They were born of practice, not theory, and were constantly under review.

Nagl's answer reminded me of the British philosopher David Hume. Hume had arrived in Oxford as a man of practical matters but quickly discovered he was more interested in books. He read what the Bodleian Library could throw at him – literature, philosophy, mathematics, history. As he delved into the world of ideas, he discovered something was missing. Real life, Hume contended, was the ultimate test of reality. His thinking injected humility into the world of abstract thought. Nagl reminded me a lot of Hume. A complex problem was solved when it passed a very simple test: people no longer found it a problem.

Will our decisions change the world for the better? Which path will lead to a more stable, prosperous world? Answering these questions is more complicated than just deferring the decision to experts. Experts, to be sure, are exceptionally important. Their data help us gain access to a world that would otherwise be invisible. But even experts are susceptible to their own myopia. Our greatest challenges in the future therefore lie much deeper.

Shortly after I returned to Australia, I was asked by friends whether my research had led me to conclude that we needed a green economy. Wasn't the world doomed unless we curtailed free markets and curbed consumption? My answer surprised them. I wasn't sure that was the real problem, I said. Maybe over-consumption was a problem – but if it was, it was a problem of the soul. As for the environment, I was much less certain.

Before we parted company, they asked me one last question: "So what's success, then, if you really want to change the world?"

I never quite worked out what I should have told my friends from the convent. All I found in Oxford was a different point of view. If there is a lesson from *Reframe*, then perhaps it is this: solving complex problems usually comes down to adjusting our focus and our definition of a solution. We are drawn to what is flashy, or noisy, or bright, but we miss what is complex, and quiet, and in the background. Grasping these things demands more patience of us, but if we get it right, we will have a real chance of changing the world for the better.

ACKNOWLEDGEMENTS

I am extremely fortunate to have met David Fickling and Chris Feik, two people who helped me enormously in writing this book. I am indebted to David for his judgement and good sense during the book's early stages. And I am indebted to Chris, my editor, for his perceptiveness and great patience in shaping this text. Their unabashed enthusiasm for the project, together with David's red socks and colourful bow ties, kept me going through its longest days.

With gratitude, I would like to acknowledge the support given to me by Olivia Pembroke and Ryan Goss. Both offered encouragement, advice, and critiqued various parts of the text. I would also like to thank Sophie Gee and Lev Grossman whose little nudges taught me a lot about writing. At Black Inc. I would like to thank the whole team for their assistance. Thanks to Sophy Williams for her expert counsel, Nikola Lusk for her way with words, and the rest of the team: Nina Kenwood, Elisabeth Young and others. I also thank Ben Naparstek and Matilda Johnson.

This book collects stories and experiences from many years and I'd like to thank all who were involved along the way. In particular I'd like to acknowledge Gordon Clark. My time at Oxford was enriched by his generosity of spirit and inquiring intellect. I would also like to acknowledge the Rhodes Trust which financially supported me at Oxford, and Magdalen College. Thanks to Don Markwell, David Clary, Sir Colin Lucas and Mary Eaton.

Several people agreed to be interviewed in one way or another for this book and I am grateful to them all. They include David Kilcullen, John Nagl, Kumi Naidoo, Raj Atluru, Karin Larsen, Mark Goldman, Derrick Lee, Shi Zhengrong, Stuart Wenham, Michael Grubb, James Cameron and others.

As the book took form, several friends and colleagues offered to read parts of the text or challenge various ideas in conversation. I'd like to thank Michael Molinari, Charles Brandon, Sam Abrams, Caitlin McElroy, Jason Pobjoy, Nicole Kuepper, Kate Robson, Jonathan Webb, Frank Jotzo, Stephen Howes, Daniel Miller, Tom Switzer, Paul Fletcher, Brett Tully, Scott Draper, Ashby Monk, Adam Dixon, Tom Spencer, Patrick Ky, Sally Halloway, Duncan Campbell, Shiro Armstrong, Peter Drysdale, Richard Chi, Claire Woods and Terry Babcock-Lumish, among others.

One person was a close witness to the writing of this script, and I owe a huge debt to Harriet for her patience and help. Finally, and above all else, I want to thank my family. I am deeply grateful for their constant love and support, without which none of this would make much sense. Thanks to Robert and my parents, to whom I dedicate this book.

INDEX